W9-DES-269

EXPERIMENTS FOR FUTURE
CHEMISTS

EXPERIMENTS FOR FUTURE
CHEMISTS

ROBERT GARDNER
AND JOSHUA CONKLIN

Enslow Publishing
101 W. 23rd Street
Suite 240
New York, NY 10011
USA

enslow.com

Published in 2017 by Enslow Publishing, LLC.
101 W. 23rd Street, Suite 240, New York, NY 10011

Library of Congress Cataloging-in-Publication Data

Names: Gardner, Robert, 1929- author. | Conklin, Joshua, author.
Title: Experiments for future chemists / Robert Gardner and Joshua Conklin.
Description: New York, NY : Enslow Publishing, 2017 | Series: Experiments for future STEM
  professionals | Includes bibliographical references and index.
Identifiers: LCCN 2016017743 | ISBN 9780766078567 (library bound)
Subjects: LCSH: Chemistry—Experiments—Juvenile literature. |Science—Experiments—Juvenile
  literature. | Science projects—Juvenile literature.
Classification: LCC QD43 .G37 2017 | DDC 540.78—dc23
LC record available at https://lccn.loc.gov/2016017743

Printed in the United States of America

To Our Readers: We have done our best to make sure all website addresses in this book were active and appropriate when we went to press. However, the author and the publisher have no control over and assume no liability for the material available on those websites or on any websites they may link to. Any comments or suggestions can be sent by e-mail to customerservice@enslow.com.

Photo Credits: Cover, blackwaterimages/E+/Getty Images (chemist), Monty Rakusen/Cultura/Getty Images (lab background throughout book), Titov Nikolai/Shutterstock.com (flask symbol), elic/Shutterstock.com (blue geometric background throughout book), Zffoto/Shutterstock.com (white textured background throughout book).

Illustrations by Joseph Hill

CONTENTS

CHAPTER 3:
CHEMICAL AND PHYSICAL CHANGES

CHAPTER 4:
ACIDS AND BASES

INTRODUCTION

Chemistry, like physics, is the study of matter and energy, but chemistry is more concerned with the properties of matter and its interactions. Organic chemistry specifically deals with the vast number of compounds (combinations of elements) that contain carbon.

Chemists are intelligent, imaginative, and creative. They enjoy analyzing and solving problems involving matter. We hope this book will help you decide if you would enjoy working as a chemist. To prepare for a career in chemistry, you should take basic and AP chemistry as well as physics and math courses offered in high school. If you do well in these courses, obtain high scores on your SATs, and ace the college admissions interviews, you will probably be admitted to a college or university where you can major in chemistry, physical science, or chemical engineering.

To help gain admission to college, you can develop interesting and challenging chemistry projects for science fairs. These projects will provide useful information for discussion as you meet college admissions directors.

Once in college, you can major in chemistry or chemical engineering. Required courses will likely include inorganic and organic chemistry, physical chemistry, analytical chemistry, physics, biology, computer science, and advanced mathematics. If your interests lie in improving the environment, you should also take courses in environmental and soil chemistry.

With a BS (bachelor of science degree) in chemistry, you could find a job in industry doing quality control or as a research assistant. However, it could be more rewarding to continue your education and obtain a PhD. Such a career path would involve research and preparing a thesis under the guidance of a chemistry professor.

The PhD would prepare you to teach and do research at a college or university, or carry on research at a chemical company. This path would require four to five years of classes and research. Your interests would likely link you with an already established professor helping him or her carry on research. It will also involve publishing original papers, but your advising professor can suggest research that will lead to findings you can publish.

Once you have your PhD, you can find work with the government, in industry, or teaching at a college or university. If you choose the academic path, you'll have more freedom to do research of your own choosing.

WHAT DO CHEMISTS DO?

Chemists experiment with matter and seek to understand a particular chemical, discover new substances, create new compounds (combinations of elements such as carbon and hydrogen), and improve the quality of existing compounds.

Many chemists analyze substances. They find out the amounts and types of chemicals in a substance. They might, for example, determine the mercury content in drinking water or in a species of fish.

Chemists may try to create new substances, such as a new plastic or paint, or look for a better, more economical way to produce a product currently on the market. Some chemists are more theoretical. They develop and test models, called theories, to explain what goes on in chemical reactions. Others are more concerned with measuring chemical reactions. For example, they might find the melting and boiling points of a new chemical, or determine the octane rating of a new gasoline.

Chemists are also active in environmental studies. They test water, soil, and other matter to see if it contains harmful chemicals. These chemists might work for federal or state government agencies, a municipal water supply, or a similar organization with environmental concerns.

And, of course, chemists are educators. They teach in high schools and community colleges, as well as colleges and universities where they usually conduct research and work closely with graduate students.

Chemists tend to specialize in a sub-discipline of chemistry. The following are some specialties:

Analytical chemists determine what chemical elements are present in compounds, and in what ratio. They also separate and identify the chemicals present in mixtures of substances.

Biochemists investigate and experiment with chemicals and chemical reactions that take place in living organisms. They are active in genetic engineering, DNA testing, developing pharmaceutical drugs, improving agricultural crops, or searching for chemicals that could be used to cure diseases.

Forensic chemists deal with the chemistry of crimes. They might analyze a substance found at a crime scene to see if it is poisonous. They also test evidence such as blood and blood stains. Any substances related to a crime will be examined and/or tested by a forensic chemist.

Neurochemists specialize in molecules and elements found within the nervous systems of animals, including humans.

Nuclear chemists study radiation and its effects on living things to create methods for treating the harmful effects of radiation on animal tissues. They may also participate in the production and use of nuclear power, and seek new methods for storing radioactive waste.

Physical chemists conduct experiments to try to understand what happens at the atomic and molecular levels during chemical reactions. They do research leading to the creation of new substances with unique properties, including medicinal products and other beneficial chemicals.

Theoretical chemists strive to better understand chemical reactions of all kinds. They develop and test theories that relate to medical, industrial, and nuclear chemistry. Such theories might pertain to DNA, cancer treatments, and alternatives to traditional fuels such as coal and oil.

BEFORE YOU BEGIN EXPERIMENTING

At times, as you do the experiments and other activities in this book, you may need a partner to help you. Try to work with someone who also enjoys experimenting. In that way, you will both enjoy what you are doing. If any safety issues or danger is involved in doing an experiment, you will be warned. In some cases, to avoid danger, you will be asked to work with an adult. Please do so. We don't want you to take any chances that could lead to an injury.

Like any good scientist, you will find it useful to record your ideas, notes, data, and conclusions in a notebook. By doing so, you can keep track of the information you gather and the conclusions you reach. It will allow you to refer to things you have done and help you in doing future projects.

THE SCIENTIFIC METHOD

Many chemists involved in scientific research are seeking answers to complex problems. They ask questions, make careful observations, and conduct research. Different areas of chemistry use different approaches. Depending on the problem, one method is likely to be better than another. Developing a new medicine, finding safer ways to use radiation, or searching for contaminants in a municipal water supply require different techniques, but they all rely on an understanding of how science is done.

Despite the differences, all scientists use a similar general approach while conducting and reporting their experimental research, called the scientific method. In most experiments, some or all of the following steps are used:
- Making an observation
- Formulating a question

- Making a hypothesis (one possible answer to the question) and a prediction (an if-then statement)
- Designing and conducting one or more experiments
- Analyzing the results in order to reach conclusions about the prediction
- Accepting or rejecting the hypothesis

Scientists share their findings by writing articles about their experiments and results. Their writings are reviewed by other scientists before being published in journals for wider circulation.

You might wonder how to start an experiment. When you observe something in the world, you may become curious and ask a question. Your question, which could arise from an earlier experiment or from reading, may be answered by a well-designed investigation. Once you have a question, you can make a hypothesis. Your hypothesis is a possible answer to the question (what you think will happen). Once you have a hypothesis, it is time to design an experiment to test a consequence of your hypothesis.

In most cases, it is appropriate to do a controlled experiment. This means having two groups that are treated exactly the same except for the single factor being tested. That factor is called a variable. For example, suppose your question is: "Is chemical X a cure for disease Y?"

You would establish two groups of patients both of whom have disease Y. One group would receive chemical X. A second group would unknowingly be given what is known as a placebo—a pill known to have no effect on the disease. If neither group shows any improvement, it is clear that chemical X is not a cure. If the group receiving the medicine is cured of the disease, then the experiment would be ended. The group not receiving the medicine could then be given the medicine so that they, too, could be cured.

Two other terms are often used in scientific experiments—dependent and independent variables. The dependent variable depends on the value of the independent variable. For example, the area of a plot of land depends on the length and width of the plot. Here, the dependent value is the area. It depends on the length and width, which are the independent variables in this example.

The results of one experiment can lead to a related question. They may send you in a different direction. Whatever the results, something can be learned from every experiment.

SAFETY FIRST

Safety is important in science and engineering. Certain rules apply when doing experiments. Some of the following rules may seem obvious to you, others may not, but it is important that you follow all of them.

1. Have an adult help you whenever this book, or any other, so advises.
2. Wear eye protection and closed-toe shoes, not sandals. Tie long hair back.
3. Do not eat or drink while experimenting. Never taste substances being used (unless instructed to do so).

4. Do not touch chemicals with your bare hands. Use tools, such as spatulas, to transfer chemicals from place to place.

5. The liquid in some thermometers is mercury (a dense liquid metal). It is dangerous to touch mercury or breathe mercury vapor. Mercury thermometers have been banned in many states. When doing experiments that require you to measure temperature, use only electronic or non-mercury thermometers, such as those filled with alcohol. If you have a mercury thermometer in the house, ask an adult if it can be taken to a local thermometer exchange location.

6. Do only those experiments that are described in this book or those that have been approved by an adult.

7. Maintain a serious attitude while conducting experiments. Never engage in horseplay or play practical jokes while conducting experiments.

8. Before beginning an experiment, read all the instructions carefully and be sure you understand them.

9. Remove all items not needed for the experiment from your work space.

10. At the end of every activity, clean all materials used and put them away. Then wash your hands thoroughly with soap and water.

The chapters that follow contain experiments and information that every young chemist should know. They will also help you to decide if being a chemist is a career you would like to pursue.

CHAPTER ONE

CHEMISTRY IS ABOUT MATTER

Early Greek philosophers believed all matter was made up of four basic elements: earth, air, fire, and water. These elements, mixed in different substances, had the effect of dryness, coldness, hotness, and wetness. The percentage of each element was different in different substances.

The idea that matter consisted of a combination of earth, air, fire, and water led to alchemy, the notion that matter could be transmuted, or changed. Alchemists, the people who practiced alchemy, believed they could transmute matter from one form to another. This belief led alchemists to try to convert less valuable metals, such as lead, into gold, which they regarded as the "perfect" form of matter. The value of gold inspired their research.

They never succeeded. However, their work led to many useful techniques, such as growing crystals and purifying liquids through distillation and filtering. Chemists still use these techniques today. Alchemists also discovered a number of substances that we recognize as true elements: phosphorus, antimony, bismuth, and zinc, among others. They identified many compounds, such as salts, acids, bases, and alcohols.

By the seventeenth century, the alchemists' failure to transmute substances into gold led many to abandon the search. However, some alchemists went on using practical techniques, which led to what we now call chemistry. These chemists realized that most matter, such as rocks, dirt, and sea water, are mixtures. Mixtures, they found, can be separated into substances whose characteristic properties (density, solubility, boiling temperature, etc.) are unchanging. They discovered these pure substances were of two kinds, elements and compounds. Elements, such as hydrogen and oxygen, could not be decomposed into simpler substances. Compounds such as water, on the other hand, could be broken down into separate elements. Our modern view of matter is the same.

Most matter comes to us in mixtures. To find out what substances are in the mixture, we must first separate the mixture into its components. Then we have the task of identifying those substances we separated. But how?

The elements and compounds extracted from a mixture are identified by their properties. Some of these properties, which distinguish one substance from another, include:

- State (solid, liquid, or gas)
- Density
- Boiling and freezing temperatures
- Solubility in water and other liquids
- Conductivity (of heat and electricity)
- Color of light emitted when heated

EXPERIMENT 1

SEPARATING THE COMPONENTS OF A MIXTURE

Separating and identifying the components of a mixture is a common task for chemists. In this experiment, you will first make a mixture and then find ways to separate it into its components.

THINGS YOU WILL NEED

- an adult
- plastic cup
- paper
- teaspoon
- sawdust
- salt
- sand
- iron filings (if available) or steel wool (without soap) cut into small pieces
- magnet
- drinking glass
- water
- Pyrex beaker or a small baking dish
- pot holder
- oven
- funnel
- filter paper or white coffee filter
- ring and ring stand or some other way of supporting a funnel

1. In a plastic cup, mix together a teaspoonful of sawdust, salt, sand, and iron or steel wool filings.
2. Spread the solids out into a thin layer on a sheet of paper.
3. Pass a magnet over the mixture. Is any component of the mixture attracted to the magnet? If it is, remove that solid from the mixture and place it on a separate piece of paper.
4. Pour the remaining mixture into a glass, add some water and stir. Do any components of the mixture dissolve in the water? Do any of the components float on the surface of the water?
5. Which component can you easily separate at this stage? How will you do it? Remove that component from the mixture and place it on a piece of paper to dry.
6. Can you separate the remaining components by pouring off the liquid into a Pyrex beaker or a small baking dish?
7. Spread out the remaining solid on a sheet of paper.
8. **Ask an adult** to place the container that holds the liquid in a warm (120°F) oven where the liquid can evaporate.
9. After the water has evaporated, use a pot holder to remove the beaker or dish from the oven. What do you find in the beaker or dish?
10. Let the mixture finish drying.

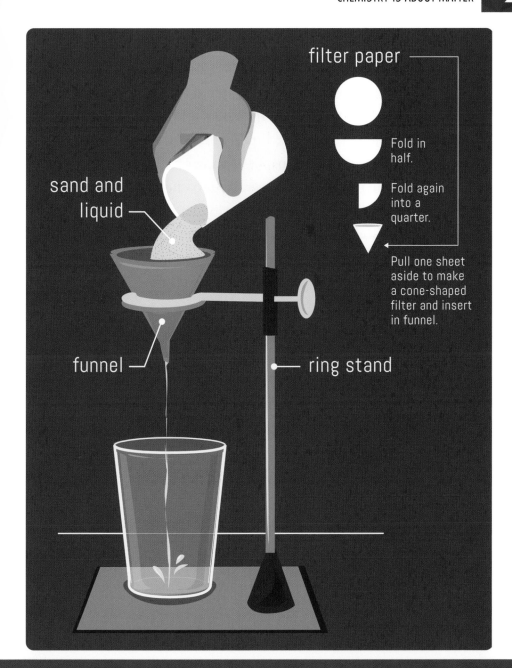

sand and liquid

filter paper

Fold in half.

Fold again into a quarter.

Pull one sheet aside to make a cone-shaped filter and insert in funnel.

funnel

ring stand

Figure 1. Filtering will separate solids from liquids.

Examine the solid sand after it has dried. Is there any evidence of salt crystals among the grains of sand? If there is, pour the sand into a glass or beaker, add water, and stir to dissolve the salt. Pour the liquid and sand into a funnel lined with a piece of filter paper as shown in Figure 1. If you don't have the round filter paper used in chemistry courses, you can use a white coffee filter. A ring and ring stand borrowed from a science room, or some other means such as a board with a hole in it, can be used to support a funnel. Collect the liquid that passes through the filter paper in a glass or beaker. Rinse the sand remaining on the paper by pouring water over it. Once the liquid has passed through the filter, dry the liquid and sand as before.

When the liquid has evaporated and the sand has dried, examine the sand and the beaker or glass again. Have you finally separated all the components of the original mixture?

EXPLORING ON YOUR OWN

About 3.5 percent of sea water is salt. If you can obtain some sea water, design an experiment to separate the water from the salt. Then, **under adult supervision,** do the experiment.

EXPERIMENT 2

THE STATES OF MATTER: SOLID, LIQUID, GAS, AND PLASMA

Matter is anything that has mass (weight). Matter can exist as a solid, a liquid, a gas, or a plasma. A plasma is gas that contains charged particles such as electrons and ions. We will not explore plasma in this book.

Solids, such as wooden blocks, have a definite size and shape. Liquids, such as water, have a definite volume but take the shape of the vessel they are in. Gases, such as air, have neither a definite shape nor volume. They fill any container they are in.

At the atomic or molecular level, the particles that make up a solid are in fixed positions and very close to one another. In a liquid, the particles touch and can move around one

THINGS YOU WILL NEED

- **an adult**
- **safety glasses**
- **ice cubes**
- **small cooking pan**
- **stove**
- **cold water**
- **glass vessel such as Pyrex glass coffee pot**
- **oven mitts**
- **one-gallon clear plastic bag that can be sealed (those with a one-zip slider work well)**
- **microwave oven with window**
- **large syringe without a needle**
- **a solid, such as a wooden block**

another. In a gas, the particles are far apart and can move in any direction.

Let's do an experiment with ice cubes. Like all solids, ice cubes have a definite size and shape.

1. Put on **safety glasses**. You will be near heated substances that might spatter.
2. Put a few ice cubes into a small pan. **Under adult supervision,** gently heat the pan on a stove. What happens to the ice?
3. As the **adult** continues heating the pan, do bubbles of gas begin rising in the liquid? What happens when they reach the surface?
4. When the liquid is boiling, it is changing to an invisible gas. The molecules of water are far apart, but their composition (H_2O) is the same.
5. Pour a cup of cold water into a container.
6. Let the **adult** hold the container of cold water above the boiling water. What collects on the bottom of the container? The gas (steam) is condensing (returning to the liquid state as it cools). How could you change the liquid water into a solid?
7. Have the **adult** continue heating the pan for a while. As you can see, it would take a long time to change all the liquid to a gas. A lot of heat (the heat of vaporization) is needed to change liquid water to a gas. In fact, 540 calories are needed to

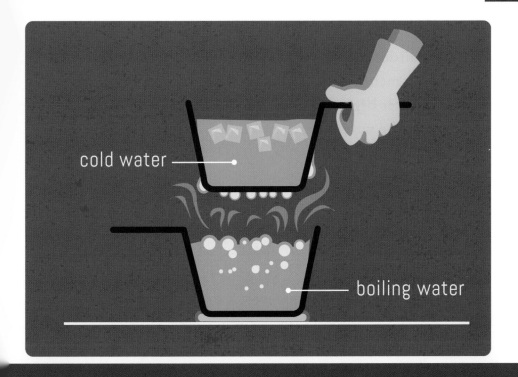

cold water

boiling water

Figure 2. You can change water from a gas into a liquid by cooling the gas.

change one gram of water to a gas at water's boiling point (212°F/100°C).

8. There is another way to show that boiling water changes into a gas. Find a one-gallon clear plastic bag that can be sealed. Put an ice cube in the bag. Flatten and roll the bag to remove most of the air. Then seal the bag so nothing can get in or out.

9. Place the bag in a microwave oven that has a window. **Ask an adult** to turn on the oven for twenty-second intervals. Watch what happens

through the window. How much time is needed to melt the ice? How much time passes before the water begins to boil? What happens to the volume as the water boils?

10. Stop heating when the bag is full. Keep the oven closed for several minutes. What happens as the gas cools?

11. Pull the piston of a large syringe part way out (Figure 3). This will draw air into the cylinder section of the syringe. Put your finger firmly over the

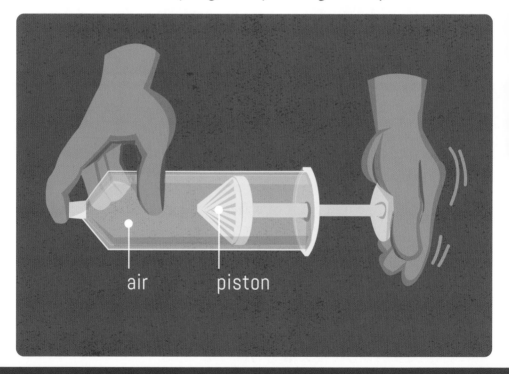

Figure 3. What happens to the volume of an enclosed gas when the pressure increases?

open end of the syringe. Push the piston inward. Can you squeeze (compress) the gas into a smaller space? Can you make the volume bigger by pulling the piston outward?

12. Can you compress a liquid into a smaller volume? Use your syringe to find out.

13. Can you compress a solid?

PHYSICAL CHANGES

Changing solid ice to liquid water, and then to gaseous water, did not change the chemical makeup of water. You were able to condense the gas and turn it back to liquid water by cooling it. You could have turned the water back to ice by cooling it more.

Changes that do not lead to a change in the chemical makeup of matter, such as changes of state or dissolving salt or sugar in water, are called physical changes.

If you were to somehow change water into the elements of which it is made, hydrogen and oxygen, that would be a chemical change. Completely new substances would have formed, and the water would have at least partially disappeared.

EXPLORING ON YOUR OWN

Do an experiment to find out at what temperature water (a liquid) changes to ice (a solid).

EXPERIMENT 3

WATER TO ICE: SOME STRANGE BEHAVIOR

THINGS YOU WILL NEED

- **ice cube**
- **small drinking glass**
- **water**
- **small jar such as a baby food jar**
- **clay**
- **food coloring**
- **transparent plastic drinking straw**
- **marking pen**
- **freezer**

Usually, solids, liquids, and gases contract (shrink) when cooled and expand when heated. Most substances continue to contract as they change from liquid to solid while freezing. And contraction continues as the solid is cooled further.

There are rare exceptions to this behavior. You can observe one very common exception in the experiment below.

1. Place an ice cube in a glass of water. Does the ice sink or float? What does this tell you about the density (compactness) of ice as compared with the density of water?

   Based on what you have seen, predict what will happen to the volume of water as it changes to ice.
2. To assess your prediction, place a lump of soft clay in a small jar.

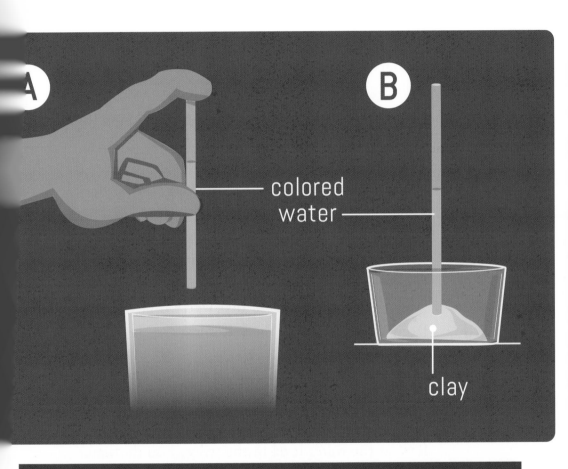

Figure 4. What happens to its volume when water freezes? How does this affect its density?

3. Color some water in a small glass by adding a few drops of food coloring.

4. Put a transparent plastic drinking straw in the water and stir.

5. Place your finger firmly on the top of the immersed straw. Then remove some water by keeping your finger firmly on top of the straw, as shown in Figure 4a. Water will remain in the straw when you lift it out of the glass.

6. Keeping your finger firmly on the top of the straw, carry the water to the small jar that contains a lump of clay. Press the bottom of the straw into the clay. When you remove your finger from the straw, the water should remain in the straw (Figure 4b).

7. When you are convinced that water is not leaking from the straw, mark the water level in the straw with a marking pen.

8. Place the jar that holds the clay and water-filled straw into a freezer.

9. After about 30 minutes, open the freezer and look at the water level in the straw. Has the water turned to ice? What happened to the volume as the liquid water changed to solid ice? Did the experiment confirm your prediction?

EXPERIMENT 4

MASS OF ICE BEFORE AND AFTER MELTING

As you have seen, volume increases when water freezes. It decreases when it melts. Does its mass change as well?

You can find out by doing an experiment.

THINGS YOU WILL NEED

- **balance that can measure mass to at least ± 0.1 gram**
- **small container with sealing cover**
- **ice cube**
- **paper towel**

1. Add an ice cube to a small container. Seal it with the cover.

2. Use a balance to find the mass of the ice and its container. Record the mass. If you notice condensation on the outside of the container, wipe it away before weighing.

3. After the ice has melted (if the container is not transparent, you can tell by shaking it), determine the mass again. If you notice condensation on the outside of the container, wipe it away before weighing. Was there any change in mass when the ice changed to water?

CONSERVATION OF MASS

You probably found that the mass did not change when the ice melted. This is but one example of thousands of experiments that demonstrate that mass is conserved. During any change of state or chemical reaction, as long as nothing is allowed to enter or leave, there is no change in mass. In other words, mass is conserved.

ANTOINE LAVOISIER, A GREAT CHEMIST

Many of the experiments that led to the law of conservation of mass were performed by French scientist Antoine Lavoisier (1743–1794). Lavoisier had the good fortune to marry Marie-Anne Paulze, a woman who illustrated his books, translated books and letters for him, helped him with experiments, and recorded his notes. Marie Lavoisier was one of the few women involved in science prior to the late nineteenth century.

Antoine Lavoisier lived during the French Revolution, a violent time in France. To support his experimental work, Lavoisier worked as a tax collector. Being a tax collector was a dangerous profession, as many, Lavoisier included, were persecuted and arrested. When Lavoisier pleaded that he was a scientist and not a tax collector, the radical judge replied, "The Republic has no need of scientists." And on May 8, 1794, Lavoisier and his father-in-law (also a tax collector) were beheaded.

One of Lavoisier's friends, astronomer Joseph Louis Lagrange, spoke for the future when he said of Lavoisier: "It took but a moment to cut off his head; it will take a century to produce another like it."

CONSERVATION OF MASS AND ENERGY

The only exception to the law of conservation of mass occurs in nuclear reactions. An example is the fission of uranium atoms into smaller atoms, which occurs in nuclear reactors that generate power. It also occurs during the fusion of hydrogen atoms to form helium, which takes place in stars such as the sun or an explosion of a hydrogen bomb.

Let's assume there is a loss of mass of a tenth of a gram—1.0×10^{-1} g or 1.0×10^{-4} kg—during a nuclear reaction. As Albert Einstein discovered, the lost mass is changed to energy according to the now famous equation $E = mc^2$, where m is the mass lost and c is the speed of light (3×10^8 m/s). This means the tiny bit of mass lost would result in the release of a quantity of energy equal to:

$$1.0 \times 10^{-4} \text{ kg} \times (3 \times 10^8 \text{ m/s})^2 = 9 \times 10^{12} \text{ joules,}$$
$$\text{or } 2.15 \times 10^{12} \text{ calories}$$

That is enough heat to melt 2.7×10^7 kg or 30,000 tons of ice.

Because of Einstein's work, we now combine the laws of conservation of mass and energy. The law now states that the total amount of mass and energy in the universe is constant.

SCIENTIFIC NOTATION AND POWERS OF TEN

In the previous section, numbers were written in scientific notation. This is something every future chemist should be comfortable doing. Writing numbers in scientific notation avoids listing the many zeros in very small or very large numbers, which are not rare in chemistry. Instead of writing 10,000,000, we can simply write 10^7.

When you multiply numbers using powers of ten, you simply add the exponents to obtain the answer. Thus, $10^3 \times 10^5 = 10^8$ and $10^3 \times 10^{-5} = 10^{-2}$.

When you divide numbers written in powers of ten, you subtract exponents. Thus,

$$10^4/10^3 = 10^1 = 10, \ 10^5/10^8 = 10^{-3}, \ 10^2/10^{12} = 10^{-10},$$

and $10^5/10^5 = 10^0 = 1$.

Remember, any number to the zero power equals 1.

Any number can be written as the product of a number between 1 and 10 and a power of ten. For example, 35,000 can be written as 3.5×10^4, 0.0025 can be written as 2.5×10^{-3}. Numbers in scientific notation can be multiplied and divided as shown here.

$$6 \times 10^7/3 \times 10^4 = 2 \times 10^3 \text{ and } 4.0 \times 10^3 \times 5.2 \times 10^{-6} = 20.8 \times 10^{-3} = 2.1 \times 10^{-2}.$$

SIGNIFICANT FIGURES

In the last number, 2.1×10^{-2}, you may wonder why the coefficient was written as 2.1 instead of 2.08. The reason is that the 2.08 was obtained by multiplying 4.0 by 5.2. Those numbers had only two significant figures. Whoever made those measurements, if he or she was paying attention to significant figures, had to estimate the 0 in 4.0 and the 2 in 5.2. The device used to make the measurements, perhaps a ruler, did not allow the person measuring to make any estimates beyond the 0 and the 2. Therefore, any numbers beyond 4.0 and 5.2 would be meaningless and not significant.

Scientific notation allows you to remove any doubt about the number of significant figures and the number of zeros that have meaning. For example, how many significant digits are there in the number 5,700 cm²? If only the 5 and the 7 had meaning, it should be written as 5.7×10^3 cm². If the first zero could be estimated, it should be written 5.70 $\times 10^3$ cm². If all four numbers were significant (only the second zero was estimated), it would be correct to write it as 5.700×10^3 cm².

Any calculation using measured numbers should have as many significant figures as the least accurate measurement. For example,

$$\frac{6.34 \text{ g}}{5.7 \text{ mL}} = 1.112 = 1.1 \text{ g/mL}.$$

CONVERSIONS

It would be ideal if the metric system, which is used throughout most of the world, were adopted by the United States. However, chemists work in the real world so you may need to convert units from one system to another.

The conversion of units can be done quite easily using unit analysis. For example, suppose you want to convert 10 miles to kilometers. The value won't change if you multiply by one, and since 1.6 km = 1.0 mi, we can multiply 10 mi by a fraction equal to one, and not change its value; consequently,

$$10 \text{ mi} \times \frac{1.6 \text{ km}}{1.0 \text{ mi}} = 16 \text{ km}.$$

Or, suppose you want to change 980 centimeters to meters, the same method can be used.

$$980 \text{ cm} \times \frac{1.00 \text{ m}}{100 \text{ cm}} = 9.8 \text{ m}.$$

Some common conversions within and between English and metric systems of measurement are given in Table 1.

Table 1. Some common conversions within and between English and metric systems of measurement.

Length in English	Length in Metric	Length, English to Metric
80 ft = 1 mi = 320 rods	1 km = 1,000 m	1.0 mi = 1.6 km
.5 ft = 1.0 rod = 5.5 yd	10 mm = 1.0 cm	1.0 in = 2.54 cm = 25.4 mm
36 in = 3.0 ft = 1.0 yd	100 cm = 1.0 m	39.37 in = 3.28 ft = 1.00 m
Area in English	**Area in Metric**	**Area, English to Metric**
43,560 ft² = 1.0 acre	10,000 m² =1.0 hectare	1.0 acre = 0.405 hectare 2.471 acres = 1.0 hectare
Volume in English	**Volume in Metric**	**Volume, English to Metric**
16 oz = 1 pt = 0.5 qt	1,000 cm³ = 1,000 mL = 1.0 L	1 qt = 0.946 L = 946 mL 1 gal = 3.785 L

DENSITY, A PROPERTY OF MATTER

Density is the mass of a sample of matter divided by its volume. In mathematical terms:

$$density = mass/volume$$

As you might expect, the density of most solids and liquids is greater than the density of gases. Let's begin by measuring the density of water. The density of water is sometimes used as a standard. The specific gravity of a substance is defined as the density of the substance divided by the density of water when both substances are at the same temperature and pressure.

Specific gravity of substance X = density of X/density of water.

EXPERIMENT 5

USING DENSITY TO MAKE PREDICTIONS

THINGS YOU WILL NEED

- ruler
- wood block
- balance good for weighing objects to ± 0.1 gram
- water
- 100-mL graduated cylinder or metric measuring cup
- dish towel
- cooking oil

Density is useful in identifying substances. In some cases, the volume of a solid object can be found by measuring its dimensions. For example, you can use a ruler to measure the dimensions of a wooden block. As you probably know, the volume of such a block is equal to its length times its width times its height.

1. Find a block of wood, determine its volume, and then weigh it.
2. Use the data to calculate its density.
3. Weigh and record the mass of a 100-mL graduated cylinder.
4. Add 100 mL of water to the graduated cylinder. Be sure the water's meniscus just touches the 100 mL line. (See Figure 5.)

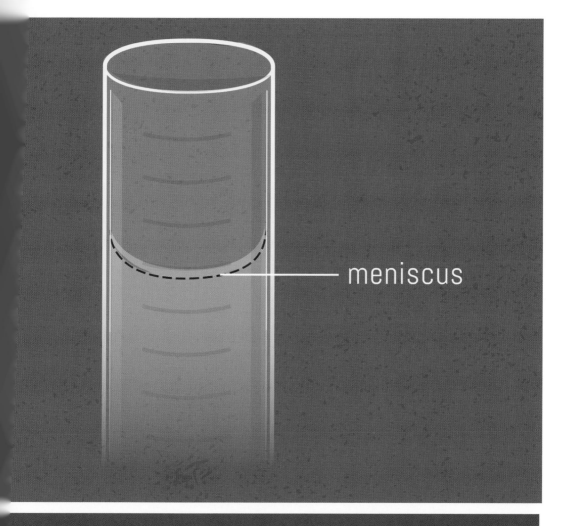

meniscus

Figure 5. The meniscus is the curved surface of the upper edge of the water in the cylinder. It forms because water adheres to glass, so the water in contact with the glass is "pulled" upward.

5. Reweigh the cylinder and water. What is the mass of the water?
6. Calculate and record the density of water.
7. Compare the densities of the wood and water. If you put the wood in water, do you think it will sink or float?
8. Put the wood block in a pan of water. Were you right?
9. Dry the graduated cylinder.
10. Add approximately 50 mL of cooking oil to the graduated cylinder. Record the volume of the oil.
11. Weigh the cylinder and cooking oil. Record the mass of the cooking oil.
12. Calculate the density of the cooking oil.
13. Make a prediction. If you add a drop of cooking oil to a glass of water, will the oil sink or float? Try it! Were you right?

    What can you say about the solubility of cooking oil in water?

EXPERIMENT 6

THE DENSITY OF STEEL

The volumes of irregular solids, such as stones, cannot be easily measured. But their volumes can be found by displacing water. Then, with their weight known, their density can be calculated.

The volumes of liquids and gases are usually measured in liters (L) or milliliters (mL). The volumes of solids are commonly measured in cubic centimeters (cm³). For your information, a milliliter and a cubic centimeter are the same volume.

THINGS YOU WILL NEED

- **steel objects such as washers, nuts, or bolts**
- **balance that can weigh to ± 0.1 gram**
- **graduated cylinder**
- **cubes or cylinders of known metals, such as aluminum, copper, iron, lead, and zinc (optional)**
- **brass object**

Let's find the density of steel. We'll use steel washers, nuts, bolts, or nails. The volume of a number of these steel pieces can be obtained by displacing water.

1. To find the density of steel, gather a large number of

steel washers, nuts, or bolts and weigh them. Record their mass.

2. Then carefully slide them into a 100-mL graduated cylinder that holds, say, 50 mL of water. If the water rises to the 85-mL line, you know the volume of the steel is 35 cm³ (85 mL - 50 mL). Once you know the volume, you can calculate the density.

3. Like many metal products, steel is an alloy, a combination of metals. Steels are primarily iron, but they contain small amounts of carbon (a nonmetal) and possibly other metals that include nickel, chromium, molybdenum, vanadium, and tungsten. By how much does the density of the steel you measured differ from the density of iron given in Table 2?

4. If possible, obtain some cubes or cylinders of known metals, such as aluminum, copper, iron, lead, and zinc. (Your school's science department may have samples that you could borrow.)

5. Find the densities of these metals and compare your findings with the densities listed in Table 2. How closely do your results agree with those in the table?

EXPLORING ON YOUR OWN

- Do different kinds of wood, such as pine, oak, maple, birch, and so on, have different densities? Design and carry out an experiment to find out.

Table 2. Densities of some liquids, solids, and gases.

Liquids	Density (g/mL)
Acetone	0.79
Ethanol	0.79
Isopropanol	0.79
Methanol	0.79
Water	1.00
Mercury	13.6
Solids	**Density (g/cm³)**
Aluminum	2.7
Copper	8.9
Gold	19.3
Iron	7.9
Lead	11.3
Lithium	0.53
Nickel	8.9
Silver	10.5
Water (ice)	0.92
Zinc	7.1
Gases (at 20°C and atmospheric pressure)	**Density (g/mL)**
Carbon dioxide	0. 0018 (1.8 g/L)
Oxygen	0.0013 (1.3 g/L)
Nitrogen	0.0012 (1.2 g/L)
Helium	0.00017 (0.17 g/L)
Hydrogen	0.000084 (0.084 g/L)

- Find some pieces of copper (pipe, nails, or tubing), aluminum (bars, nails, tubing, or flashing), lead and zinc (flashing), and so on. Find the densities of these metals. Then decide whether they are pure metals or alloys.
- Do an experiment to determine whether nickels (5-cent coins) are really made of nickel.
- Brass is an alloy of copper and zinc. Find a brass object. Determine its density. Use Table 2 to determine the approximate percentage of zinc and copper in the brass.

DENSITY OF GASES

To find the density of a gas, a chemist might first remove the air from a flask using a vacuum pump. The evacuated flask would be weighed. Then the gas whose density was to be determined would be allowed to enter the vacuum through a valve, and its pressure adjusted to the pressure of the atmosphere. The flask would be reweighed and the mass of the evacuated flask would be subtracted leaving the mass of the gas. Dividing the mass of the gas by the flask's volume would reveal the gas's density.

As you can see from Table 2, gas densities are very small. For that reason, gas densities are often given in grams per liter (g/L). Gas densities depend on pressure and temperature. Doubling the pressure on a gas, as you might guess, doubles its density because doubling the pressure halves its volume. This is known as Boyle's Law: The volume of a gas, at constant temperature, is inversely proportional to its pressure. It is named for Robert Boyle (1627–1691), who discovered this relationship through experimentation.

Gas densities also vary with temperature because gases expand when warmed and shrink when cooled. Gas volumes are directly proportional to the absolute temperature, sometimes measured in Kelvins. Zero degrees Kelvin (K) is equal to -273° Celsius. This is called absolute zero because it's the coldest temperature possible. At this temperature, the speed of atoms and molecules is essentially zero.

Gas volumes at constant pressure are proportional to the absolute temperature. Doubling the absolute temperature of a gas will double its volume if the pressure remains unchanged. If, at constant pressure, the temperature of a gas increases from 0°C to 273°C, its volume will double because the absolute, or Kelvin temperature, has doubled from 273K to 546K, or from 273°C to 546°C. The relationship between gas volume and absolute temperature is known as Charles's Law. It is named for Jacques Charles (1746–1823), who discovered the relationship in about 1787.

If you try to weigh a gas in air, the gas is buoyed up by the weight of the air it displaces. Since the density of air at room temperature is about 1.20 g/L, any liter of gas you weigh in air will appear to have a mass that is 1.20 grams less than its actual mass.

EXPERIMENT 7

THE DENSITY OF A GAS

As you have seen, it is difficult to measure the mass of a gas. Gases have very small densities because a gas is mostly empty space. Gas molecules are about ten times farther apart in all three directions than those of a solid or liquid. As a result, gas densities are about 1/1000 the densities of solids and liquids.

THINGS YOU WILL NEED

- **seltzer tablet**
- **balance that can measure to ± 0.1 g or better**
- **twist tie**
- **test tube**
- **graduated cylinder or metric measuring cup**
- **heavy drinking glass**
- **water**
- **pen or pencil**
- **notebook**
- **rubber tubing (about 50 cm long)**
- **one-hole rubber stopper to fit test tube**
- **glass tube about 10 cm long to fit into rubber stopper**
- **large bottle [500 mL–1 L (1 pint –1 quart)]**
- **plastic pail**
- **square piece of cardboard or glass to cover mouth of bottle**

Is there any way to measure the density of a gas if you don't have sophisticated equipment such as vacuum pumps? In some cases, the answer is yes. For example, seltzer tablets react with water to form a gas. If you weigh the water and seltzer tablet before and after the reaction, any loss of mass should be because of the gas that escapes. By collecting the gas, you can measure its volume. Knowing the mass and volume, you can find its density.

1. To carry out this experiment, break a dry seltzer tablet in half. Put the pieces on a balance pan.

2. Also, depending on the type of balance you are using, figure out a way to find the mass of a test tube that holds about 10 mL of water as well as that of the seltzer tablet. Record the combined mass of tablet, test tube, and water in your notebook.

3. Set up the apparatus shown in Figure 6. A heavy drinking glass can support the test tube. Fill the large bottle with water. Fill the pail about one-third of the way with water.

4. Cover the mouth of the bottle with a cardboard square. Hold the square against the bottle as you turn it upside down and put its mouth under the water in the pail. Remove the square. The water will stay in the bottle.

5. Place the rubber tubing (about 50 cm long) inside the large bottle of water, through the top.

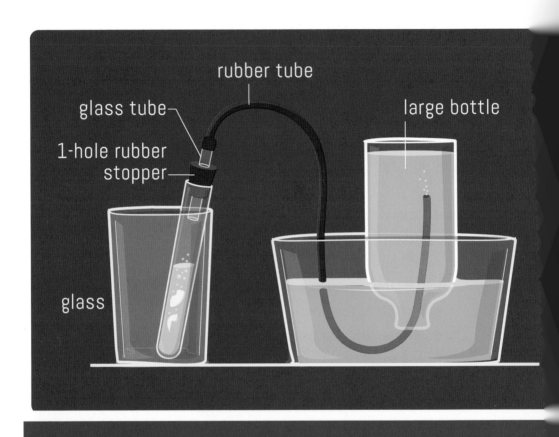

Figure 6. Find the density of a gas.

6. Drop the pieces of tablet into the water in the test tube and immediately insert the one-hole rubber stopper into the mouth of the test tube. The glass and rubber tubes now connect the two containers. The gas produced in the test tube will travel through the tubing to the bottle where it will collect as it displaces water from the bottle.

7. Let the reaction proceed for about ten minutes. By that time the reaction will be nearly complete.

8. Remove the rubber tube that extends to the top of the large bottle before you remove the rubber stopper from the test tube. Otherwise, air may flow through the tubing into the bottle.

9. Cover the mouth of the bottle with the piece of cardboard and remove it from the pail. Turn the bottle right-side up and remove the square.

10. Use a graduated cylinder or metric measuring cup to find the volume of gas that was produced. How can you find the volume?

11. How can you find the mass of the gas? Record that mass in your notebook.

12. Using the mass and volume of the gas, determine the density of the gas. Could the gas be any of those shown in Table 3?

Table 3. Density of six common gases at room temperature (20°C) and air pressure at sea level.

Gas	Density (g/L)
Air	1.20
Carbon dioxide (CO_2)	1.84
Helium (He)	0.154
Hydrogen (H_2)	0.083
Nitrogen (N_2)	1.16
Oxygen (O)	1.33

EXPLORING ON YOUR OWN

• Do an experiment to show that air weighed in air has no mass.

CHAPTER TWO

ATOMS, IONS, AND MOLECULES

Early in the nineteenth century, chemist John Dalton (1766–1844) crafted a theory to explain the laws of chemistry. Like other chemists of that time, Dalton knew that elements were pure substances and that different elements could combine to form compounds. To explain what matter is made of, Dalton developed the atomic theory. He proposed that all matter is made up of tiny, indestructible particles called atoms. According to his theory, the atoms of any one element are identical but differ from the atoms of any other element. Atoms of different elements differ in weight. And, since atoms are indestructible, there is no change in weight when substances undergo physical or chemical change.

To find the relative weights of atoms, he decomposed compounds into their separate elements and weighed each element. He also weighed the elements and then combined them to form a compound. For example, by passing an electric current through water, he decomposed the water into hydrogen and oxygen. This resulted in the release of eight grams of oxygen for every one gram of hydrogen. If one gram of hydrogen was mixed with eight grams of oxygen and ignited with a spark, an explosion took place. After the explosion, nine grams of water had formed and no gas remained. Based on this evidence, Dalton concluded that oxygen atoms weighed eight times as much as hydrogen atoms. He assumed that hydrogen and oxygen atoms combined to form water in a 1:1 ratio. He concluded that the molecular formula for water was HO.

Later, an Italian chemist, Amedeo Avogadro (1776–1856), hypothesized that equal volumes of gases at the same temperature and pressure contain the same number of molecules. Since for any given volume of oxygen, twice that volume of hydrogen combines with it, Avogadro concluded that the formula for water was H_2O. Today we know that Avogadro was right. However, it took half a century before his hypothesis and conclusion about the formula for water was accepted by most chemists.

Since hydrogen is the lightest (least dense) gas known, chemists assigned hydrogen atoms a relative mass of one unit (1 amu, or 1 atomic mass unit). No one knew what the actual mass of an atom was. Atoms had far too little mass to be weighed. However, if hydrogen atoms weigh 1 amu, oxygen atoms must weigh 16 amu. After all, two grams of hydrogen combines with 16 grams of oxygen, a ratio of 1:8. Since two atoms of hydrogen combine with one atom of oxygen, the oxygen atoms must be 16 times as heavy as the hydrogen atoms in order for their weight ratio in water to be 1:8.

$$\frac{2 \times 1}{16} = \frac{2}{16} = \frac{1}{8}$$

Today, we know not only the relative mass of the atoms of every element, we know their actual mass as well. The relative and actual masses of some common elements are shown in Table 4.

Table 4. The relative and actual weights of the atoms of some common elements.*

Relative mass of atoms*	Actual mass in multiples of 10^{-24} g**	Element in atomic mass units (amu)
Hydrogen	1.0	1.7
Helium	4.0	6.7
Carbon	12.0	20
Oxygen	16.0	27
Sodium	23.0	38.3
Magnesium	24.3	40.5
Aluminum	27.0	45
Sulfur	32.1	53.5
Chlorine	35.5	59
Iron	55.8	93
Copper	63.5	106
Zinc	65.4	109
Lead	207	345

* Based on oxygen atoms having an atomic mass of 16 amu.
** A septillionth of a gram is 0.000000000000000000000001 gram.

EXPERIMENT 8

A MODEL OF ATOMS, MOLECULES, AND COMPOUNDS

In this experiment and the next one, we will use paper clips and washers to represent atoms of two imaginary elements, C and W.

THINGS YOU WILL NEED

- **box of large, identical paper clips**
- **paper**
- **identical steel washers**

1. Pour several large, identical paper clips onto a sheet of paper. Let the paper clips represent "atoms" of an "element" represented by the symbol C.

2. Pour several small, identical steel washers onto a sheet of paper. Let the washers represent "atoms" of an "element" represented by the symbol W. Notice that all the "atoms" of C are identical. All the "atoms" of W are also identical. But, clearly, the atoms of C are different than the atoms of W.

3. Assume element C reacts with element W to form the compound CW. Join some atoms of C with some atoms of W to form molecules of the compound CW.

   In what ratios, other than 1:1, might atoms of C and W combine?

EXPERIMENT 9

PAPER CLIPS, WASHERS, "CHEMICAL FORMULAS," AND LAWS OF NATURE

In this experiment, you will use the paper clips to represent atoms of element C and washers to represent atoms of element W. You will combine them to form molecules of compounds made from the atoms.

THINGS YOU WILL NEED

- **large, identical paper clips**
- **identical steel washers**
- **balance that can weigh to at least ± 0.1 g**
- **notebook**
- **pen or pencil**
- **calculator (optional)**

1. Prepare a large number of "molecules" (at least ten) of the compound CW by joining "atoms" of C and W, some of which are shown in Figure 7a. Place all the molecules on a balance pan. Record the weight of the "compound" you have prepared. (If you don't have a balance, assume that atoms of C weigh 1.8 g and that atoms of W weigh 0.6 g.)

2. Next, "decompose" the compound into the elements C and W as shown in Figure 7b. Place the atoms of both elements on the same balance you used before. What is the total weight of the elements?

3. Compare the total weight of the two elements with the weight of the compound you prepared. How do your results illustrate the law of conservation of matter? That is, how do they illustrate the fact that matter is neither created nor destroyed?

4. Now weigh separately each of the elements that you obtained by decomposing the compound. What is the weight of C? What is the weight of W? What is the relative weight of an atom of C to an atom of W? For example, if you found 12 grams of washers had combined with 36 grams of large paper clips, the relative weight of a large paper clip (C) to a washer (W) would be:

$$36/12 = 3/1 \text{ or } 3:1.$$

If the mass of an atom of W is considered to be 10 amu, what is the mass of an atom of C in amu?

5. Repeat the experiment, but prepare only about two-thirds as many molecules of the compound CW. Again, record the weight of the "compound." Then decompose the compound into the elements C and W. What was the weight ratio of C to W in the compound?

How do the results of these two experiments illustrate the law of definite proportions? That is, how do the results demonstrate that elements

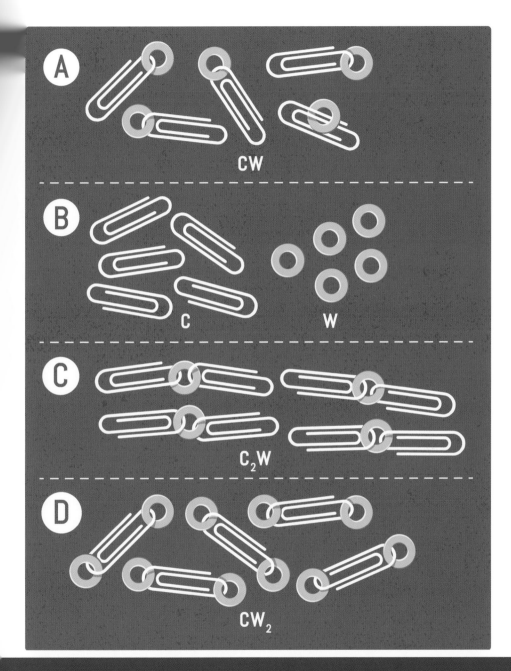

Figure 7. a) "Molecules" of CW. b) "Atoms" of the decomposed "compound" CW. c) "Molecules" of C_2W. d) "Molecules" of CW_2.

always combine to form a compound in a fixed ratio by weight?

6. Prepare as many molecules as possible of the compound C_2W (two C atoms and one W atom per molecule). See Figure 7c. The formula C_2W shows that there are two atoms of C and one atom of W in each molecule of C_2W.

7. Place all the molecules of C_2W on a balance pan. Record the weight of the "compound" you have prepared. (If you don't have a balance, assume that atoms of C weigh 1.8 g and that atoms of W weigh 0.6 g.)

8. "Decompose" the compound into the elements C and W. Place the atoms of both elements on the same balance pan you used before. What is the total weight of the elements? Compare the total weight of the two elements with the weight of the compound you prepared.

9. Next, weigh the elements C and W separately. What is the weight ratio of C to W in this compound?

10. Prepare as many molecules as possible of the compound CW_2 (two W atoms and one C atom per molecule). See Figure 7d. The formula CW_2 shows that there are two atoms of W and one atom of C in each molecule of CW_2.

11. Repeat steps 2, 3, and 4 for the compound CW_2.

12. You have now prepared three different compounds of the elements C and W: CW, C_2W, and CW_2.

What is the weight ratio of C to W in CW to the ratio of C to W in C_2W? For example, suppose the weight ratio of C to W in CW is 3/1, and in C_2W the weight ratio of C to W is 6:1. Then the weight ratio of C to W in CW to the ratio of C to W in C_2W is 3/6, or 1/2, or 0.5.

What is the weight ratio of C to W in CW to the ratio of C to W in CW_2?

THE LAW OF MULTIPLE PROPORTIONS

You have just discovered the law of multiple proportions, another discovery that led Dalton to the atomic theory. The law of multiple proportions states that if two elements form more than one compound, the weight ratio of the elements in one compound will be a simple multiple of the weight ratio in the other compound or compounds.

For example, chemists found that carbon and oxygen combine to form two different gases. In one, carbon monoxide, the weight ratio of oxygen to carbon is 4:3. In the other, carbon dioxide, the ratio is 8:3. The weight ratio of oxygen in carbon dioxide to oxygen in carbon monoxide is 8:4, or more simply 2:1.

Whenever two elements combine to form more than one compound, the law of multiple proportions holds true. As another example, hydrogen and oxygen combine to form two compounds, water (H_2O) and hydrogen peroxide (H_2O_2). As you know, the weight ratio of oxygen to hydrogen in water is 8:1. What is the weight ratio of oxygen to hydrogen in hydrogen peroxide? How do these two compounds illustrate the law of multiple proportions?

Dalton knew that elements sometimes combine to form more than one compound because he had investigated the gaseous compounds formed when nitrogen and oxygen combine.

Results similar to his are found in Table 5.

Examine the third column of Table 5. It shows the weight of oxygen in each compound that combines with a fixed weight (10 g) of nitrogen. Examine the last column of Table 5. It shows the ratio of the weight of oxygen in each of three compounds to the weight of oxygen in N_2O. N_2O has the least oxygen per 10 g of nitrogen. What would be the weight ratio of W_2/W_4? Of W_2/W_1?

Table 5. Compounds of nitrogen and oxygen.

Compound Name	Chemical Formula	Weight, W, of oxygen united with 10 g of nitrogen	Weight ratios W/W_3
Nitrogen oxide	NO	$W_1 = 11.43$ g	$W_1/W_3 =$ 11.43/5.72 = 2/1
Nitrogen dioxide	NO_2	$W_2 = 22.86$ g	$W_2/W_3 =$ 22.86/5.72 = 4/1
Dinitrogen oxide	N_2O	$W_3 = 5.72$ g	--
Dinitrogen trioxide	N_2O_3	$W_4 = 17.15$	$W_4/W_3 =$ 17.15/5.72 = 3/1

EVIDENCE FOR ATOMS AND MOLECULES

The laws of definite proportions and multiple proportions can best be explained by assuming three things: (1) Matter is made up of atoms. (2) The atoms of an element are identical. (3) The atoms of an element are different from the atoms of any other element, especially in weight.

There is much more evidence to support the atomic theory. You will discover some of that evidence in the rest of this book.

WHEN IS A MOLE NOT AN ANIMAL?

Early chemists could not weigh individual atoms or molecules. They did, however, figure out a way of knowing when they had equal numbers of atoms or molecules. Look back at Table 4. There you see the relative weights of atoms expressed in atomic mass units. The table shows that oxygen atoms are 16 times as heavy as hydrogen atoms. Therefore, chemists knew that if they had one gram of hydrogen and sixteen grams of oxygen, then they had equal numbers of atoms of both elements. These chemists may not have known how many atoms of each element they had, but they knew the numbers were equal because the ratio of the elements, 1:16, was the same as the ratio of their atomic masses.

Chemists defined the mole as: the atomic or molecular weight of an element or compound expressed in grams.

Therefore, the weight of one mole of water is 18 grams because one molecule of water, H_2O, consists of two atoms of hydrogen and one atom of oxygen. The atomic weight of hydrogen is 1 and the atomic weight of oxygen is 16. Thus, $2 \times 1 + 1 \times 16 = 18$.

What is the weight of a mole for each of the substances listed below?

- Aluminum (Al)
- Aluminum oxide (Al_2O_3)
- Helium (He)
- Magnesium (Mg)
- Sodium chloride (NaCl)
- Sucrose (sugar) ($C_{12}H_{22}O_{11}$)
- Zinc chloride ($ZnCl_2$)

Often chemicals are dissolved in water to form solutions. The concentrations of such solutions are expressed in terms of their molarity, or moles per liter.

If one mole of ordinary salt, sodium chloride (NaCl), is dissolved in a liter of solution, the concentration of the solution is one molar (1 M). A mole of salt contains 58.5 grams of salt. Remember, Na = 23 amu and Cl = 35.5 amu.

EXPERIMENT **10**

THE SOLUBILITY OF SODIUM CHLORIDE

Let's find the solubility of sodium chloride; that is, let's find the number of grams of salt that will dissolve in 100 grams of water.

THINGS YOU WILL NEED

- **water**
- **graduated cylinder**
- **beaker or drinking glass**
- **paper**
- **balance that can weigh to at least ± 0.1 g**
- **notebook**
- **pen or pencil**
- **2 small spoons**
- **kosher salt (because it has no additives)**

1. Add 100 mL (100 g) of water to a gradu-ated cylinder.
2. Pour that water into a beaker or glass.
3. Fold a small piece of paper and place it on the pan of a balance. Weigh and record the mass of the paper.
4. Use a spoon to slowly and carefully add exactly 100 grams of kosher salt to the paper. (Kosher salt has none of the additives in ordinary table salt.)
5. Slowly add the salt you weighed to the water. Stir each small addition of salt with a spoon until the salt completely dissolves (disappears). When the solution is nearly saturated (holds all the salt

possible) and requires much stirring to dissolve the salt, add only tiny amounts of salt.

6. When no more salt will dissolve, the solution is saturated. For our purposes, we'll ignore any small amount that remains.

7. Reweigh the paper and any remaining salt. How much salt dissolved?

   What is the solubility of sodium chloride in grams per 100 grams of water at room temperature and one atmosphere of pressure?

   What is the molarity of the solution you made? Remember: molarity is measured in moles per liter.

EXPLORING ON YOUR OWN

- Does temperature affect the solubility of sodium chloride? Does it affect the solubility of sugar? Do experiments to find out.
- If possible, obtain some sea water. Find a way, **under adult supervision**, to determine the molarity (moles per liter) of salt in sea water. Sea salt is primarily sodium chloride.
- Design and carry out experiments to find the freezing temperatures of saturated solutions of kosher salt, Epsom salt, and sugar.

EXPERIMENT

SOLUBLE OR INSOLUBLE?

Not all substances are soluble in water. A first test is often used to find out whether a substance is soluble in water or some other liquid, such as alcohol. If a small amount of a substance dissolves (disappears) when mixed in a liquid, we say it is soluble in that liquid. If little or none of the solid dissolves, we say it is insoluble. In this experiment, you'll decide whether each of a number of solids are soluble or insoluble in water.

1. Try dissolving, in turn, a small amount (1/4 teaspoonful) of as many of the following as are

THINGS YOU WILL NEED

- **teaspoon**
- **sugar**
- **drinking glasses**
- **graduated cylinder or metric measuring cup**
- **water**
- **kosher salt**
- **small amounts of such substances as sugar, baking soda, baking powder, flour, instant tea, instant coffee, Kool-Aid, Tang, vitamin C, aspirin, gelatin, Epsom salt, corn starch**
- **citric acid**
- **methanol (methyl alcohol)**
- **Epsom salt (magnesium sulfate)**

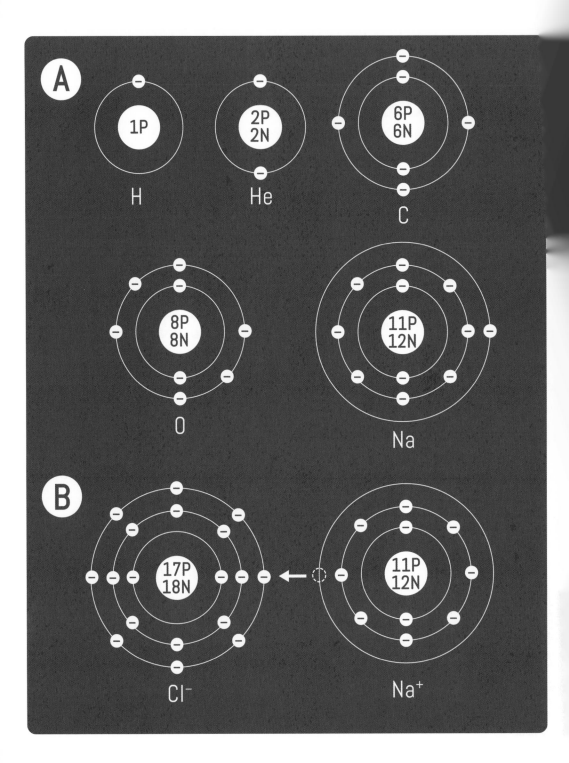

available in half a glass of water: sugar, baking soda, baking powder, flour, instant tea, instant coffee, Kool-Aid, Tang, vitamin C, aspirin, gelatin, Epsom salt, and powdered starch.

Which substances are soluble in water? Which are insoluble? Are any of the insoluble substances soluble in hot water? Have an adult help you test this.

WHICH SUBSTANCES CONDUCT ELECTRICITY?

All atoms consist of a tiny nucleus with protons and (except for hydrogen) neutrons (Figure 8a). Early in the history of chemistry, chemists discovered that molten (melted) salts such as sodium chloride (NaCl), potassium iodide (KI), and others would conduct electricity. To explain this behavior, a young Swedish chemist named Svante Arrhenius (1859–1927) proposed in 1884 that salts consist of ions— atoms that carry an electric charge. You may know that electric charges can flow between the positive and negative electrodes of a battery. Ions, Arrhenius proposed, can carry charge from one electrode to the other.

Figure 8. a) The structure of several atoms are shown. Notice that the number of protons and electrons in an atom are equal. Notice, too, that the electrons of an atom orbit the nucleus at different distances. A maximum of two electrons are found in the first orbit, and eight in the second orbit. More than eight are possible in orbits farther out. b) If a sodium atom transfers its outermost electron to a chlorine atom, two ions are formed—a sodium ion (Na^+) and a chloride ion (Cl^-)—the ions found in table salt.

In the case of sodium chloride, the salt is made up of positive sodium ions (Na^+) and negative chloride ions (Cl^-). (See Figure 8b.) When an electric current is passed through molten sodium chloride, sodium metal collects at the negative electrode, and chlorine gas bubbles off the positive electrode.

Most chemists did not accept Arrhenius's theory. It wasn't until J. J. Thomson (1856–1940) discovered the electron (an elementary particle with a negative charge) in 1897, and certain elements, such as uranium, were found to give off charged particles (radiation), that Arrhenius's idea became widely accepted. It became clear that atoms contained charged particles in the form of negative electrons and positive protons, and could form ions by gaining or losing electrons. A chloride ion was an atom with one extra electron; a sodium ion was an atom that had lost one electron. In recognition of his work, Arrhenius was awarded the Nobel Prize in Chemistry in 1903.

EXPERIMENT **12**

IONS AND AN ELECTRIC CURRENT

When you hear the word "salt," you probably think of the white crystals you shake onto food to add flavor. To a chemist, however, a salt is a compound that consists of positive and negative ions. For example, table salt—sodium chloride—consists of equal numbers of positive sodium ions (Na^+) and negative chloride ions (Cl^-). Calcium chloride ($CaCl_2$) has two singly charged chloride ions (Cl^-) for every one doubly charged calcium ion (Ca^{+2}). Aluminum ions carry an excess of three positive charges (Al^{+3}). What would be the chemical formula for aluminum chloride?

Will ordinary solid salt, the kind you put on food, conduct electricity?

> ### THINGS YOU WILL NEED
>
> - **table salt**
> - **clear plastic vial**
> - **paper clips**
> - **6-volt dry-cell battery, or 4 D-cells, masking tape, and a mailing tube**
> - **flashlight bulb and socket**
> - **wires with alligator clips**
> - **water**
> - **Epsom salt**
> - **coffee stirrer or swizzle stick**
> - **sugar**

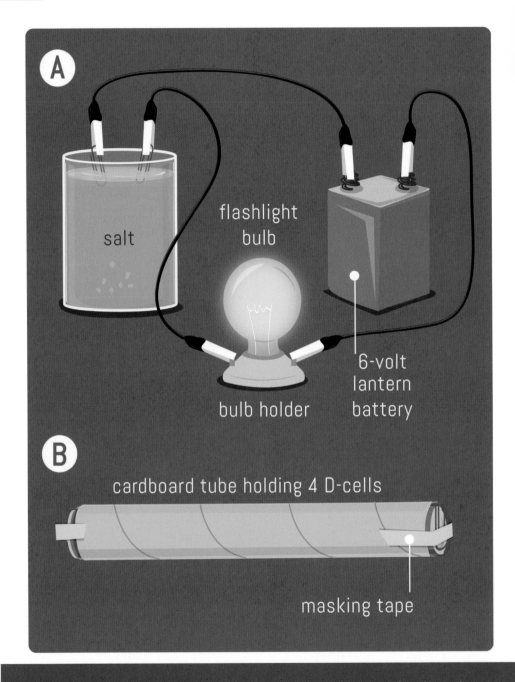

Figure 9. Does salt conduct electricity? How about a salt solution?

1. To find out, nearly fill a clear plastic vial with table salt.

2. Add two paper clips as shown in Figure 9a. Most of the clip's surface should be immersed in the salt. Connect them to a 6-volt lantern battery through a flashlight bulb set in a socket. The connections can be made with wires that end in alligator clips as shown. (If you don't have such a battery, you can make one by placing four D-cells head to tail in a mailing tube (Figure 9b). The tube should be slightly shorter than the total length of the four D-cells. Use masking tape to fasten paper clips firmly against the positive and negative terminals as shown.

   If you don't have a bulb holder, touch the metal base of the bulb with one wire and the metal side with a second wire. If you don't have wires with alligator clips, you can use clothespins to connect the wires.

   Does the bulb light? Does solid table salt conduct electricity? Do you think a salt solution will conduct electricity?

3. To find out, remove half the solid salt from the vial. Then add water to nearly fill it, and stir with a wooden coffee stirrer to dissolve as much of the salt as possible.

4. Again, connect the paper clips on the vial to the battery and a light bulb as shown in Figure 9a.

Does the bulb light now? What does this tell you?

You won't find sodium collecting at the negative electrode. If it did, it would react with water to release hydrogen. The chemical reaction of sodium with water is:

$$Na + H_2O \rightarrow H_2 + Na^+ + OH^-.$$

What do you see that indicates a gas is being released at the negative electrode? What might that gas be?

Chlorine is very soluble in water. Why will you not see a gas collecting at the positive electrode?

Epsom salt, so named because it was first obtained from mineral springs in Epsom, England, is magnesium sulfate. Magnesium sulfate ($MgSO_4$) crystals contain equal numbers of magnesium (Mg^{+2}) and sulfate (SO_4^{-2}) ions. Each of these ions carries two electric charges. Do you think a solution of Epsom salt will conduct an electric current?

5. Fill the vial you used before about halfway with Epsom salt. Add water until the vial is nearly full and stir.

6. Then connect the vial's paper clip electrodes to the 6-volt battery through the light bulb. Does the flashlight bulb glow? Did you predict the result?

What about substances that do not have ions, such as sugar? The molecular formula for ordinary

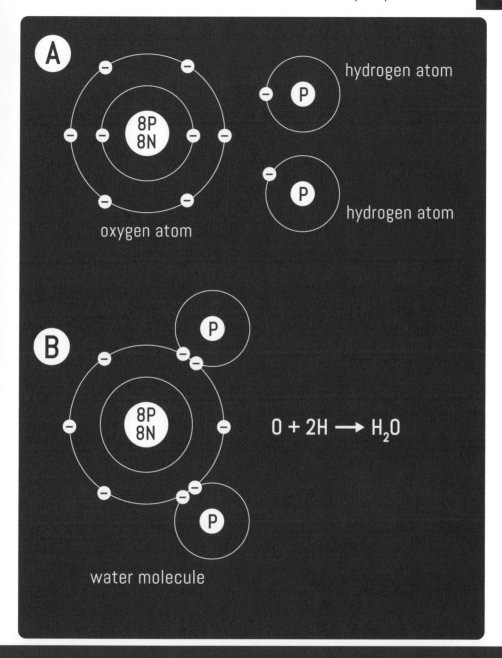

Figure 10. Oxygen atoms have a nucleus containing eight protons and eight neutrons (atomic mass = 16 amu). In this model, the electrons (negatively charged particles) orbit the positively charged nucleus like planets orbiting the sun. The first orbit can hold only two electrons, the second can hold up to eight electrons. Oxygen has six electrons in orbit two. Hydrogen atoms have only one electron. By sharing electrons with two hydrogen atoms, oxygen fills its second orbit with eight electrons, and both hydrogen atoms fill their first orbit with two electrons.

		Lewis diagrams	Structural formula
A	Water (H_2O)	$2\,H\bullet + \overset{\circ}{\underset{\circ\circ}{\circ\,O\,}}_{\circ}^{\circ} \longrightarrow H \overset{\bullet\bullet}{\underset{\circ\circ}{\circ\,O\,}}_{\circ}^{\circ}$	$\begin{array}{c} H \\ | \\ H{-}O \end{array}$
B	Ammonia (NH_3)	$3\,H\bullet + \overset{\circ\circ}{\underset{\circ}{\circ\,N\,\circ}} \longrightarrow H\overset{\circ\circ}{\underset{\circ\circ}{\circ\,N\,\circ}}H$ H	$\begin{array}{c} H \\ | \\ H{-}N{-} \\ | \\ H \end{array}$
C	Methane (CH_4)	$4\,H\bullet + \bullet\overset{\bullet\bullet}{\underset{\bullet}{C}}\bullet \longrightarrow H\overset{\bullet\bullet}{\underset{\bullet\bullet}{\circ\,C\,\circ}}H$ H	$\begin{array}{c} H \\ | \\ H{-}C{-}H \\ | \\ H \end{array}$
D	Carbon dioxide (CO_2)	$\bullet\overset{\bullet\bullet}{\underset{\bullet}{C}}\bullet + 2\,\overset{\circ\circ}{\underset{\circ\circ}{\circ\,O\,}}_{\circ} \longrightarrow \overset{\circ\circ}{\underset{\circ\circ}{O}}::C::\overset{\circ\circ}{\underset{\circ\circ}{O}}$	$O{=}C{=}O$

table sugar (sucrose), is $C_{12}H_{22}O_{11}$. Do you think
it will conduct electricity when dissolved in water?

7. To find out, fill the vial you used before about
halfway with sugar. Add water until the vial is
nearly full.

8. Stir to make a solution of sugar.

9. Connect the paper clip electrodes to the battery and
light bulb. Does the sugar solution conduct electricity? Was your prediction correct?

COVALENT BONDING

As you found, sugar solutions do not conduct electricity.
Sugar, like many other compounds, does not consist of ions.
Instead, these compounds are formed when atoms share
electrons. Such bonding between atoms is called covalent
bonding.

For example, water, H_2O, is a covalent compound.
Figure 10 shows how oxygen and hydrogen form two covalent bonds to form water. Hydrogen atoms have a nucleus
that contains a single proton. (All protons have a single

Figure 11. Many compounds are formed by covalent bonds. Lewis diagrams are
named in honor of Gilbert Newton Lewis (1875–1946), an American chemist who
suggested that the electron arrangements of atoms can be used to predict what
chemical reactions may take place. These Lewis diagrams show how electron sharing form covalent bonds to produce water, ammonia, methane, and carbon dioxide.
Shared electrons can also be represented by lines as shown under structural formu-
las. Double bonds form where four electrons are shared, as in carbon dioxide. There
are also triple bonds where six electrons are shared.

positive charge.) The electron that lies in an orbit outside the hydrogen nucleus bears a negative charge so the atom is neutral.

Figure 11 shows how water, ammonia, methane, and carbon dioxide are bonded covalently. In Lewis diagrams, electrons are represented by small circles or dots. (Some chemists use circles and Xs.) The different symbols are used to show that the bonding electrons are from atoms of different elements.

Carbon dioxide and methane are organic molecules. They contain carbon. As you can see in Figure 11, carbon forms double covalent bonds with oxygen in carbon dioxide molecules. Covalent bonds are very common among organic compounds as well as many inorganic (noncarbon) compounds, such as ammonia.

POLAR AND NON-POLAR COMPOUNDS

> ## THINGS YOU WILL NEED
>
> - **plastic comb**
> - **paper towel or wool cloth**
> - **water faucet**
> - **cooking oil**
> - **sink**
> - **finishing nail**
> - **Styrofoam cups**
> - **ethanol (optional)**

As you have learned, covalent compounds consist of atoms that share electrons. In some compounds, the atoms do not share the electrons equally. They tend to be more concentrated at one end of the molecule than the other. This is true of water molecules. As shown in the diagram of a water molecule (Figure 12a), the angle between the two covalent bonds that join the hydrogen atoms to the oxygen atom is 105 degrees. However, the oxygen atom has a stronger attraction for electrons than do the hydrogen atoms. As a result, the oxygen end of the molecule is slightly negative while the hydrogen end has a slight positive charge. On account of this, we say the molecule is polar. Because water molecules are polar, the hydrogen (+) end of the molecule is attracted to the oxygen (-) end of other water molecules. As

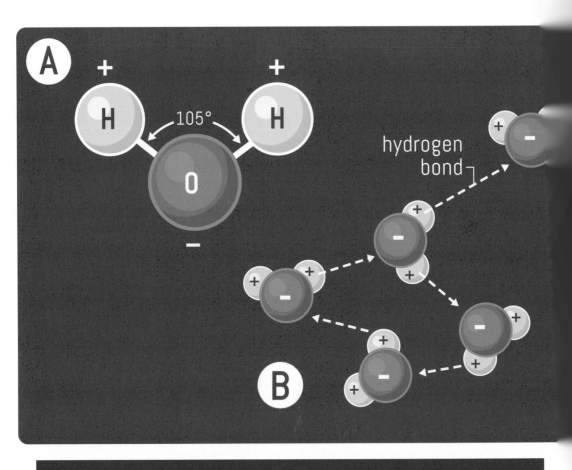

Figure 12. a) In water molecules, hydrogen atoms bond to oxygen atoms at an angle of 105 degrees. b) The polar molecules of water are attracted to one another through weak hydrogen bonds.

illustrated in Figure 12b, these attractive forces create weak bonds, called hydrogen bonds, between water molecules.

In this experiment, you will observe the effects of water's polarity.

1. Give a plastic comb an electric charge by rubbing it with a paper towel or a wool cloth.

2. Bring the comb near a thin stream of water flowing from a faucet. What happens to the stream? Would it make any difference whether the comb was positively or negatively charged? (Hint: Look again at Figure 12.)

3. Over a sink, repeat the experiment with a thin stream of cooking oil. To obtain a thin stream of cooking oil, first, use a finishing nail to make a small hole in the bottom of a Styrofoam cup.

4. Have a partner hold the cup with their finger over the small opening while you pour some cooking oil into the cup.

5. Charge the comb as before and have your friend remove their finger so that a thin stream of oil flows into another cup below the opening.

6. Does the cooking oil stream bend when you hold the charged comb near it as shown in Figure 13? What can you conclude about the polarity of cooking oil molecules?

7. If possible, repeat the experiment using ethanol (ethyl alcohol) and a new Styrofoam cup. What happens this time? Are alcohol molecules polar?

Figure 13. Are molecules of cooking oil polar?

EXPERIMENT 14

MORE ON WATER'S POLARITY

The polarity of water molecules causes them to attract one another. The attractive forces between their molecules causes water to pull together. This tendency of water to hold together creates a skinlike surface, a property called surface tension.

THINGS YOU WILL NEED

- **clean dinner fork**
- **paper clip**
- **clean water**
- **bowl**
- **plastic vial or small glass**
- **eyedroppers**
- **waxed paper**
- **toothpicks**
- **cooking oil**

1. To see how well water holds together, use a clean dinner fork to gently place a paper clip on the surface of some clean water in a bowl. Notice that the paper clip doesn't sink. Look closely. You will see that it does bend the water's "skin."

2. To see another effect of the water's polar molecules, fill a plastic vial or small glass with water.

Then, using an eyedropper, see how high you can heap the water above the edge of the vessel.

3. For still another effect of water's polarity, use a clean eyedropper to place a drop of water on a sheet of waxed paper. Notice the round shape of the drop when viewed from the side.

4. Place a second drop of water close to the first one. Then use a toothpick to move the second drop slowly closer to the first one. What happens when the two drops touch?

5. Repeat these three experiments using cooking oil in place of water. How do you expect the results to differ? How do they differ?

CHAPTER THREE

CHEMICAL AND PHYSICAL CHANGES

Let's look at two physical changes and then a few chemical changes. We'll begin with a physical change, the melting of ice. It won't come as a surprise that ice becomes water again when it melts. However, the heat needed to melt a gram of ice may surprise you.

EXPERIMENT 15

THE ENERGY (HEAT) TO MELT ICE

As you learned in chapter 1, energy (heat) is needed to change solid water (ice) to its liquid state. Use this experiment to find the quantity of heat needed to melt one gram of ice. This quantity is known as the heat of fusion.

You can measure heat in units called calories. One calorie is the amount of heat gained (or lost) when one gram of water changes its temperature by one degree Celsius. If the

THINGS YOU WILL NEED

- **100-mL graduated cylinder or metric measuring cup**
- **warm water**
- **thermometer**
- **Styrofoam cup**
- **paper towel**
- **ice**

temperature of 100 grams of water increases by 10°C, the heat transferred to the water is 1,000 calories (100 g × 10°C = 1,000 cal). If its temperature decreased by 10°C, it would have transferred 1,000 calories to something else.

1. To begin, pour 100 mL (100 g) of warm (about 30°C) tap water into a Styrofoam cup.

2. Use a paper towel to remove any cold water that may lie on the surface of a small ice cube.

3. While stirring, add the ice cube as shown in Figure 14. Continue to add small pieces of ice until the water reaches approximately 10°C. This will cool the water to a temperature about as far below room temperature as it was above room temperature when you started. In this way, the heat lost by the warm water to the cooler air, as it cools from 30° to about 20° during the first part of the experiment, will balance the heat gained from the warmer air as the water cools from 20° to 10°.

4. Pour the water, which now contains the melted ice, into a graduated cylinder. How much ice melted?

5. The heat lost by the warm water can be found from the weight of the water (100 g) and its change in temperature. In the example given, the

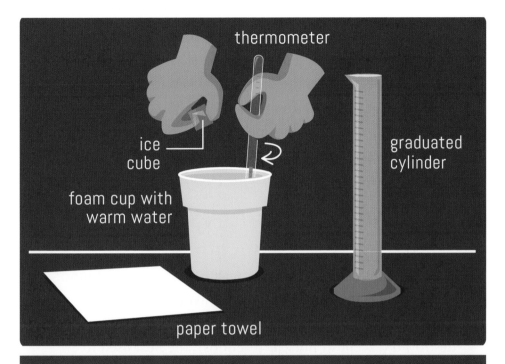

Figure 14. The materials shown here can be used to find the heat of fusion for water.

change in temperature of the warm water was 20°C (30°C - 10°C). Therefore, the warm water lost 2,000 calories because:

$$100 \text{ g} \times -20°C = -2,000 \text{ cal.}$$

However, in this experiment the heat lost by the water did *two* things: (1) It melted the ice. (2) It warmed the melted ice from 0°C to the final temperature of the water (10°C).

In the example given, suppose the final volume of water was 122 mL. Since 22 g of ice melted (122 g - 100 g), the heat required to warm the melted ice from 0° to 10°C was 220 cal (22 g × 10°C). The remaining 1,780 calories (2,000 - 220) was the heat used to melt the ice. According to this example, the heat needed to melt one gram of ice (the heat of fusion) was:

$$1{,}780 \text{ cal}/22 \text{ g} = 81 \text{ cal/g.}$$

How does this value compare with the value you found?

Millions of experiments have shown that energy, like matter, is conserved. Since energy is never created or destroyed (except in nuclear reactions), the heat used to melt one gram of ice will equal the heat released when one gram of water freezes.

EXPLORING ON YOUR OWN

- Does the shape of a piece of ice affect the rate at which it melts? Design and conduct an experiment to find out. Can you explain your results?
- You may have seen icicles form when snow melts and drips off a roof. How can water freeze to form icicles when the temperature is warm enough to melt the snow?

EXPERIMENT 16

WATER'S HEAT OF VAPORIZATION

The heat needed to change one gram of a liquid at its boiling point to a gas is called the heat of vaporization. In this experiment, you can make an estimate of water's heat of vaporization. Do you think it will be more or less than water's heat of fusion?

For safety, **wear goggles, long sleeves, and oven mitts** throughout this experiment.

Work under adult supervision during this experiment because you will be using electricity and very hot water.

The boiling point of water at sea level is approximately 100°C. That temperature remains at the boiling point as long as the water boils. The energy added to the boiling water

THINGS YOU WILL NEED

- **an adult**
- **safety goggles, long sleeves, and oven mitts**
- **200-watt electric immersion heater**
- **electrical outlet**
- **graduated cylinder or metric measuring cup**
- **12- or 14-oz Styrofoam cups**
- **beaker or can**
- **water**
- **thermometer with a range of -10–110°C**
- **watch with second hand**

does not increase the water's temperature. Just as energy is needed to separate (lift) a mass from Earth's surface, so energy is needed to separate molecules from one another.

1. Although a label on an immersion heater may read 200-W, the actual power of the heater may be somewhat higher or lower. Consequently, the first thing you should do is calibrate the heater. That is, find out how much heat the heater provides in one minute. To do this, put 200 grams of cold water in a 12- or 14-oz Styrofoam cup. If possible, use water that is 5 to 10 degrees cooler than the room. This will reduce heat losses that occur when the water temperature rises above room temperature. (Stacking two or three Styrofoam cups together will provide better insulation.)

2. Place the cups in a beaker or can to provide support so that the cups do not fall over when you place the immersion heater in.

3. Put the immersion heater in the cold water. Use a thermometer to measure the water temperature. (See Figure 15.) After recording the initial temperature of the water, record the exact time and then plug the immersion heater into an electrical outlet.

An immersion heater should not be plugged into an electrical outlet unless its coil is in water!

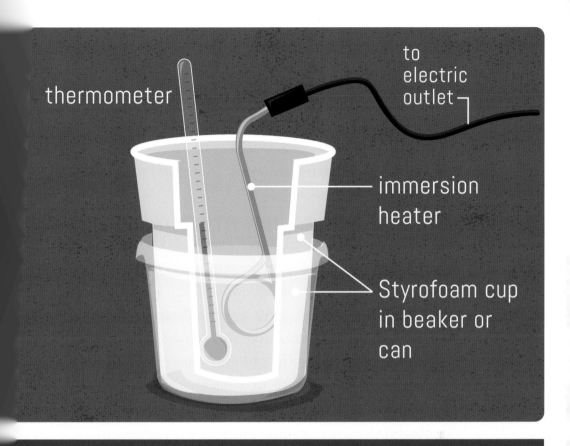

Figure 15. An immersion heater can be used to heat water and obtain an estimate of the heat of vaporization for water.

4. Stir the water gently with the thermometer as the water is heated. After exactly one minute, **ask the adult** to pull the plug (grasp it by the plug, not the cord) from the outlet to disconnect the heater.

5. Leave the heater in the cup as you stir the water to find its final temperature. Why should you leave the heater in the water after it is disconnected?

6. Record the final temperature of the water. By how many degrees did the water's temperature change?

7. Use the data you have collected to calculate how much heat, in calories, the immersion heater transferred to the water in one minute.

8. Repeat the experiment again to be sure your results are consistent.

    If the heater really delivers as much heat per second as its rating (200-W) indicates, it provides 2,870 calories per minute. How does this value compare with the value you found?

9. Now place 150 mL (150 g) of cold tap water in the insulated Styrofoam cups supported by a beaker or can. With only 150 g of water, very little will spatter from the cup when the water boils.

10. Put the immersion heater in the water, stir, and record the initial temperature of the water.

11. **Ask the adult** to plug in the heater. Allow it to transfer heat to the water for seven or eight minutes. During that period of time, a significant amount of water will boil away. Once the water is boiling, record its temperature. Why might it boil at some temperature other than 100°C?

12. After seven or eight minutes, **ask the adult** to disconnect the heater while you record the total time you have added heat to the water. Then remove the heater from the water.

13. **Ask the adult**, who is wearing oven mitts and

safety goggles, to pour the hot water into a graduated cylinder. How much water remains? What
weight of water was changed to gas?

With the data you have collected, you can make a rea-
sonable estimate of the amount of heat required to boil away
one gram of water at its boiling point. For example, suppose
that your heater transfers 3,000 cal/min. In eight minutes
it will provide 24,000 calories. If the initial temperature of
the water was 20°C and the boiling temperature was 100°C,
then 12,000 calories (150 g × 80°C) was required to bring
the water to the boiling point. Assume that the remaining
12,000 calories (24,000–12,000) was used to change liquid
water to gaseous water. If 20 g of water boiled away, then
the energy required to boil away one gram of water was:

$$12,000 \text{ cal}/20 \text{ g} = 600 \text{ cal/g}.$$

Using your data, what do you find is the heat of vaporization for water?

Again, because we know energy is conserved, you would
expect water's heat of condensation (the heat released when
gaseous water condenses to liquid water) to be the same as
its heat of vaporization, and it is. Of course, when gaseous
water condenses, heat is released. It's similar to the energy
associated with gravity. A rocket fired vertically loses its
kinetic energy as it rises and gains potential energy. As it
falls back to Earth, it loses its potential energy and regains

kinetic energy, but, of course, some of the initial kinetic energy is converted to heat because of friction with air.

Examine the heats of fusion and vaporization for the substances listed in Table 6. How do your estimates for the heats of fusion and vaporization for water compare with the values given in the table?

Table 6. Molecular weight, in atomic mass units (amu), and heats of vaporization and fusion for a few substances with molecular weights reasonably close to water's (18).

Substance	Molecular or atomic mass (amu)	Heat of vaporization (cal/g)	Heat of fusion (cal/g)
aluminum	27	2500	95
ammonia	17	329	108
copper	63.5	1150	49
ethanol	46	205	26
hydrogen	2	108	14
oxygen	32	51	3
sulfur dioxide	64	95	24
water	18	540	80

How do the heats of fusion and vaporization for water compare with those of other substances that have about the same molecular or atomic weight? How do you think your answer is related to the polarity of water molecules?

Given the information of the substances in Table 6, how do you think their melting and boiling points would compare? After giving it some thought, see Table 7 at the end of this chapter.

A chemical reaction in which oxygen combines with other substances to form compounds is called oxidation. You see oxidation every time something burns. Burning is rapid oxidation, but not all oxidation reactions are so speedy. The rusting of iron is an example of slow oxidation, which you will examine in Experiment 17.

EXPERIMENT 17

A CHEMICAL CHANGE: THE OXIDATION (RUSTING) OF IRON

THINGS YOU WILL NEED

- **safety goggles**
- **steel wool (without soap)**
- **scissors**
- **water**
- **household ammonia**
- **vinegar**
- **cups or glasses to hold liquids**
- **paper towels**
- **soap and water**

A chemical reaction in which oxygen combines with other substances to form compounds is called oxidation. The rusting of iron, which you will observe in this experiment, is an example of slow oxidation. Iron rusts when oxygen in the air slowly combines with it to form a compound called iron oxide (Fe_2O_3). As the iron combines with oxygen, a new compound is formed. This means there is a chemical change. To observe this chemical reaction, you can use steel wool, which contains iron. Air, which is 20 percent oxygen, will supply the oxygen.

1. To see how different chemicals affect the rate of the reaction, begin by cutting a steel wool pad (one without soap) into four equal parts. Soak one

piece in water, one in ammonia water, and a third in vinegar. The fourth piece can remain dry to serve as a control.

2. After soaking the steel wool samples overnight, remove them. Put them on labeled paper towels. Then wash your hands thoroughly.

3. Leave the samples for at least a day or more, but examine them periodically to see what happens. Which piece is first to show evidence of rusting? Do any appear not to rust at all?

4. While waiting, go on to the next oxidation experiment.

EXPERIMENT 18

ANOTHER OXIDATION-REDUCTION REACTION

To a chemist, oxidation is more than a reaction with oxygen. A chemist defines oxidation as a loss of electrons. A gain of electrons is called reduction. When something is oxidized (loses electrons) something else must be reduced (gain electrons).

1. Place a piece of paper on a balance pan. On the paper, weigh out 50 grams of blue copper sulfate

THINGS YOU WILL NEED

- **about 50 g of copper sulfate (borrow from science teacher or buy at a store that provides swimming pool needs)**
- **paper**
- **distilled water, rain water, or soft water**
- **glass, plastic cup, or beaker**
- **stirring rod or coffee stirrer**
- **steel nail**
- **steel wool (obtain from hardware store)**

crystals ($CuSO_4 \cdot 5H_2O$). Copper sulfate consists of copper ions (Cu^{+2}), which have a charge of +2 combined with sulfate ions (SO_4^{-2}), which carry a charge of -2.

2. Pour about 100 mL of distilled water, rain water, or soft water into a glass, plastic cup, or beaker. Add the copper sulfate and stir until most of the blue crystals dissolve.

3. Since steel is mostly iron (Fe), find a steel nail taller than the container holding the copper sulfate solution. Rub the nail with some steel wool to make it bright and shiny. Then put the nail in the copper sulfate (Figure 16a).

4. After an hour, remove the nail. Notice the reddish substance that has collected on the nail. It is copper (Figure 16b). Copper atoms (Cu) have no excess charge. The copper ions must have gained electrons to become copper atoms. The electrons

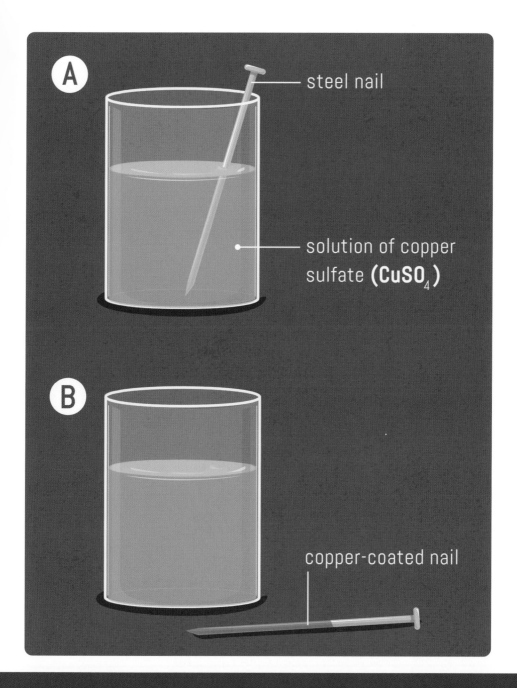

Figure 16. Oxidation of iron atoms and reduction of copper ions. a) Before the reaction. b) After the reaction.

came from the iron atoms, which were uncharged. The iron atoms, by losing electrons, became positively charged ions and dissolved in the solution. The chemical equations below summarize what happened in this oxidation-reduction reaction.

$$Fe \rightarrow Fe^{+2} + 2e-$$
$$Cu^{+2} + 2e- \rightarrow Cu$$

The net reaction is: $Cu^{+2} + Fe \rightarrow Cu + Fe^{+2}$

What was oxidized? What was reduced? (Sulfate ions are not shown because they are not involved in the reaction. Chemists call ions that are not involved in a reaction spectator ions.)

In Experiment 17, iron rusted under some conditions. The iron changed from uncharged atoms into positively charged ions. So the iron was oxidized; it lost electrons. What do you think was reduced?

ELECTRICITY FROM CHEMICALS BY OXIDATION-REDUCTION

Batteries consist of one or more electric cells. Electric cells have one thing in common; they use chemicals to produce an electric current. One D-cell (flashlight battery), for example, consists of a zinc container that serves as the negative terminal and surrounds an electrolyte, a dark, moist

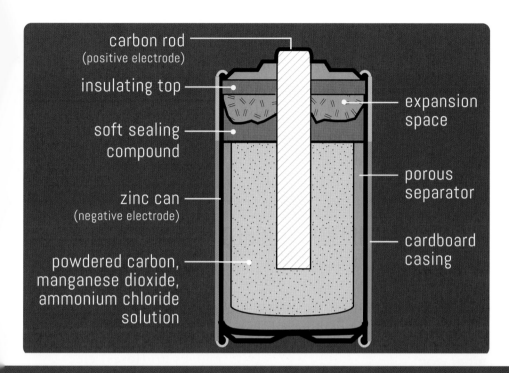

Figure 17. A cross section of a flashlight cell. A porous separator keeps the powdered carbon and manganese dioxide from coming in contact with the zinc, but allows the ammonium chloride solution to pass freely. The zinc can, which serves as the negative electrode, is enclosed in a cardboard case that holds the top insulation and insulates the zinc can from metal objects.

mixture of manganese dioxide (MnO_2), powdered carbon (C), and ammonium chloride (NH_4Cl). A solid carbon rod runs through the center of the cell and serves as the positive terminal. See Figure 17.

BUILDING AN ELECTRIC CELL

THINGS YOU WILL NEED

- science teacher or knowledge-able adult
- safety glasses
- copper and zinc plates about 3.5 cm x 10 cm (1.5 in x 4 in)
- steel wool
- 2 drinking glasses or 250-mL beakers
- copper nitrate solution: dissolve 24 g of copper nitrate, $Cu(NO_3)_2 \cdot 3H_2O$, in 200 mL of distilled water
- zinc nitrate solution: dissolve 29 g of zinc nitrate, $Zn(NO_3)_2 \cdot 6H_2O$, in 200 mL of distilled water
- ammeter (0–5 amps)
- wires with alligator clips
- voltmeter (0–3 volts)
These materials are generally found in a school science room or lab.

The source of the electric current (electrons) in an electric cell comes from the oxidation of the negative terminal. It gives up (loses) electrons to provide an electric current that flows to the positive terminal where reduction (gain of electrons) occurs.

The chemicals found in most electric cells are quite common. In fact, you can easily build one. But first, put on **safety glasses** and **ask a science**

teacher or a knowledgeable adult to oversee your work.

1. Prepare a strip of copper and a strip of zinc. The strips should be about 3.5 cm × 10 cm (1.5 in × 4 in) and they should be polished (shined) with steel wool.
2. Put the zinc strip in a glass or beaker that contains 200 mL of zinc nitrate solution.
3. Put the copper strip in a glass or beaker that contains 200 mL of copper nitrate solution.
4. Using wires with alligator clips, as shown in Figure 18, connect the zinc strip and copper strip to an ammeter (a device that measures electric current in amperes). Is there any current?
5. Next, connect the two solutions with a paper towel strip as shown. What happens when the two solutions diffuse along the towel and meet? If the ammeter needle moves below zero, reverse the wire leads to the meter. Which metal is the positive electrode? Which metal is the negative electrode?
6. Remove the ammeter. Replace it with a voltmeter (a device that measures energy per charge in volts). What is the voltage reading across this cell?

For an electric cell to work, one electrode must provide electrons; the other electrode must accept electrons. In the cell you built, the zinc provided electrons; the copper ions accepted the electrons. The reaction involved

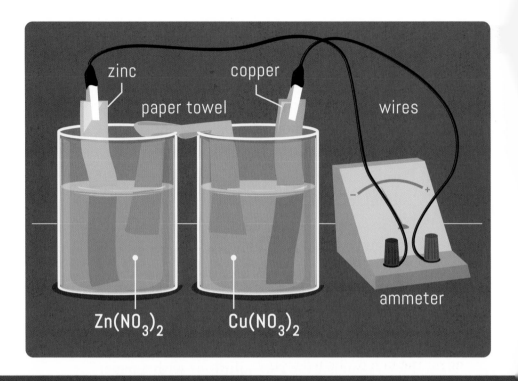

Figure 18. This electric cell uses zinc and copper as electrodes. The electrodes are immersed in electrolyte solutions of zinc nitrate and copper nitrate.

oxidation and reduction as shown by the chemical reactions below.

$$Zn \rightarrow Zn^{++} + 2\ e-$$
$$Cu^{++} + 2\ e- \rightarrow Cu$$

The net reaction is: $Zn + Cu^{++} \rightarrow Zn^{++} + Cu$

What was oxidized? What was reduced?

EXPERIMENT 20

FACTORS AFFECTING THE RATE OF A CHEMICAL REACTION

Some reactions, such as the explosion of gun powder, go quickly. Other reactions, such as the rusting of iron, go slowly. In this experiment, you will see how temperature and surface area affect the rate of the reaction between seltzer tablets and water.

THINGS YOU WILL NEED

- **seltzer tablets**
- **water**
- **ice cubes**
- **drinking glasses**
- **cold tap water**
- **graduated cylinder or metric measuring cup**
- **hot tap water**

1. Examine a package of seltzer tablets. What chemicals are in a seltzer tablet?
2. Prepare some ice water. Fill a glass two-thirds of the way with cold water. Fill much of remaining third with ice cubes.
3. After five minutes, pour 150 mL of the ice water into a glass. Pour 150 mL of hot tap water into a second identical glass.

Table 7: Molecular weight, in atomic mass units (amu), and melting and boiling points for the chemicals in Table 6.

Substance	Molecular or atomic mass (amu)	Melting point (°C)	Boiling point (°C)
aluminum	27	658	1800
ammonia	17	-77.7	-33.4
copper	63.5	1084	2310
ethanol	46	-117	78.5
hydrogen	2	-259	-253
oxygen	32	-218	-183
sulfur dioxide	64	-72.7	-10
water	18	0	100

4. Add a seltzer tablet to the cold water. At the same time, add a seltzer tablet to the hot water. How does temperature affect the speed of a chemical reaction?

5. To see the effect of surface area on the rate of a reaction, crush a seltzer tablet into tiny pieces on a piece of paper.

6. In separate identical glasses, simultaneously pour the crushed tablet and drop a whole tablet into equal amounts of cold water. What do you conclude about the effect of surface area on reaction rate?

CHAPTER FOUR

ACIDS AND BASES

Many chemicals can be identified as acids or bases. Substances that are neither acidic nor basic, such as water, are said to be neutral. The Latin word for acid, *acidus*, means sharp or sour. That is how sour tasting substances, such as vinegar, came to be known as acids. In addition to their sour taste, acids dissolve in water to form solutions that conduct electricity. Acids contain hydrogen, which is released when the acid is added to certain metals such as zinc. Acids turn blue litmus paper red, and neutralize bases. This means they can combine with bases to form a substance that is neutral; neither an acid nor a base.

Bases are also called alkalis, a word that means ashes. Ashes have properties that chemists use to identify bases; they have a bitter taste and feel slippery like soap. American pioneers made soap by boiling wood ashes with animal fat. Bases, like acids, are conductors of electricity. They turn red litmus paper blue, have a bitter taste, and neutralize acids.

Many acids and bases can conduct electricity because they form ions when dissolved in water. Acids form hydrogen ions (H+) and bases form hydroxide ions (OH-). The chemical equation below should help you understand how acids and bases neutralize one another to form water (HOH or H_2O).

$$H+ + OH- \rightarrow HOH$$
$$\text{or } H+ + OH- \rightarrow H_2O$$

If the acid is hydrochloric acid, HCl, and the base is sodium hydroxide, NaOH, then the overall reaction is:

$$H+ + Cl- + Na+ + OH- \rightarrow H_2O + Na+ + Cl-$$

If the water is allowed to evaporate, crystals of salt (sodium chloride [NaCl]) will remain.

EXPERIMENT 21

IDENTIFYING ACIDS AND BASES

Early chemists might identify acids by their sour taste and bases by their bitter taste. We don't recommend this method. There is a better way. Strips of blue and red litmus paper make it easy to identify acids and bases. Blue litmus paper turns red in an acid; red litmus paper turns blue in a base. See Figure 19.

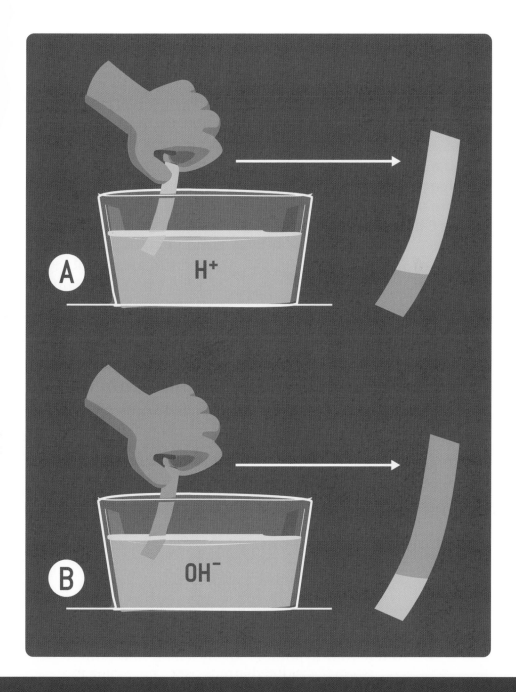

Figure 19. a) Blue litmus paper dipped in an acid (H+) turns red. b) Red litmus paper dipped in a base turns blue.

THINGS YOU WILL NEED

- an adult
- lemon juice
- red and blue litmus paper (obtain from your school's science dept. or a science store or supply house)
- 5 or 6 blackberries
- bowl
- dinner fork
- strainer
- cups or glasses
- red cabbage
- non-aluminum pan and cover
- water
- stove
- forceps
- container with cover
- refrigerator
- white vinegar
- medicine cups (30 mL) or small jars (baby food jars are good)
- glass jars or test tubes
- household ammonia solution
- substances for testing: lemon juice, apple juice, grapefruit juice, rubbing alcohol, cleanser powder, salt and sugar solutions, aspirin, wood ashes, baking soda, baking powder, lime (calcium oxide), citric acid, Kool-Aid or Tang, salt, sugar, milk of magnesia, washing soda, ginger ale, tonic water, seltzer water, pickle juice, olives

1. You can start with the old method of identifying acids and bases. Place a drop of lemon juice on your tongue. Do you think lemon juice is an acid or a base? Why?

2. To test your hypothesis about lemon juice, dip pieces of red and blue litmus paper into some lemon juice. What do you conclude?

Litmus paper is not the only way to test for acids and bases. There are many acid-base indicators. You can even make your own.

3. Put five or six blackberries in a bowl. Crush them with a fork until you have something resembling jam.

4. Pour the "jam" into a strainer and collect the dark red juice in a cup or glass. Save any of the juice you don't use in this experiment. You can use it in the next experiment to make indicator sticks.

5. Red cabbage juice makes a good acid-base indicator. Remove a few leaves from a red cabbage. Break the leaves into small pieces and place them in a non-aluminum pot. Add enough water to just cover the leaves. Put a cover on the pot and **ask an adult** to help you heat the pot until the water is boiling. Reduce the heat, but continue boiling for about half an hour. Then turn off the heat and let the water cool to room temperature.

6. Using forceps, remove the cabbage leaves. Pour the cabbage juice solution into a container. Cover it and put it in a refrigerator.

Vinegar is a solution of acetic acid ($C_2H_4O_2$), which, as you probably know, has a sour taste.

7. To confirm that vinegar is an acid, dip a piece of blue litmus paper into a few milliliters of white vinegar. Does the litmus paper turn red?

8. Add a few drops of the cabbage extract to the white vinegar in a small glass jar or medicine cup. What is the color of cabbage juice indicator in an acid?

When ammonia gas (NH_3) dissolves in water, it reacts with the water to form ammonium (NH_4^+) and hydroxide ($OH-$) ions. See the chemical equation below:

$$NH_3 + H_2O \rightarrow NH_4^+ + OH-$$

9. To confirm that an ammonia solution is basic, dip a piece of red litmus paper into a few milliliters of a household ammonia solution. What indicates that the ammonia solution is a base?

10. Next, add a few drops of the cabbage juice to a few milliliters of ammonia solution. What is the color of cabbage juice indicator in a base?

11. Add a few drops of the cabbage juice indicator to some tap water. What is the color of the indicator in a neutral solution?

12. Repeat the experiment using the berry juice extract. What is the color of berry juice indicator in an acid? In a base? In a neutral solution?

13. Using litmus paper, berry juice, and cabbage juice, test some of the following substances to determine whether each is an acid, a base, or neutral: lemon juice, apple juice, grapefruit juice, rubbing alcohol, cleanser powder (in water), salt and sugar solutions, crushed aspirin dissolved in water, wood ashes mixed with water, solutions of baking soda and baking powder, citric acid or

Kool-Aid or Tang crystals dissolved in water, milk of magnesia, washing soda dissolved in water, ginger ale, tonic water, seltzer water, pickle juice, and juice from a jar of olives.

Which of these substances are acids? Which are bases? Which are neutral?

EXPLORING ON YOUR OWN

- Turmeric, a common spice, can also be used as an acid-base indicator. Prepare an extract of turmeric by mixing 1/4 teaspoonful of turmeric with a quarter cup of rubbing alcohol. Add a few drops of the turmeric indicator to acids, bases, and neutral substances. How does it compare with other indicators you have tried?

- Investigate other common indicators that can be found in many science rooms or obtained from a science store or science supply house. These include phenolphthalein, methyl orange, methyl red, bromothymol blue, congo red, indigo carmine, and alizarin yellow. Other than color, how do they differ?

- Prepare a cup of hot tea. Add a few drops of lemon juice to the tea. What evidence do you have to suggest that tea is an acid-base indicator?

EXPERIMENT 22

NEUTRALIZATION

One characteristic of acids and bases is their ability to neutralize one another. To see the neutralization process, you can add an acid to a base, or a base to an acid.

THINGS YOU WILL NEED

- **teaspoon**
- **milk of magnesia**
- **saucer**
- **water**
- **cabbage juice extract from Experiment 21**
- **eyedropper**
- **lemon juice**

1. Pour about 1/2 teaspoonful of milk of magnesia, $Mg(OH)_2$, into a saucer. Add about two teaspoonfuls of water and stir.

2. Add several drops of cabbage juice extract and stir the mixture to obtain a uniform color.

3. Using an eyedropper, add lemon juice (citric acid) drop by drop.

4. Observe the color of the solution at the place where the drops of acid land.

5. Stir the liquid as you add the drops until you see a distinct color change. What has happened?

6. Now go the other way. Rinse your eyedropper and use it to add drops of milk of magnesia to the

solution. Do this slowly. Notice the effect of one drop on the color of the solution. Can you see an intermediate color (purple) just before the solution changes from acid to base or base to acid? Remember, cabbage juice is purple in a neutral substance. If you can see the indicator turn purple, you are witnessing the point at which neutralization occurs.

What happens to the color of the neutral solution if you add a drop or two of lemon juice? A drop or two of milk of magnesia?

STRONG AND WEAK ACIDS AND BASES

Acids such as vinegar (acetic acid) are weak acids; they provide relatively few hydrogen ions (H+) in solution. Weak bases, such as ammonia, provide few hydroxide ions (OH–) in solution. On the other hand, strong acids and bases, such as hydrochloric acid and sodium hydroxide, provide lots of ions.

The strength of an acid can be determined by its pH. The pH measures the concentration of hydrogen ions. (See Table 8.) Neutral substances, such as water, have a pH of 7. Substances with a pH less than 7 are acidic; substances with a pH greater than 7 are basic. A solution with a pH of 1 is very acidic; one with a pH of 5 is mildly acidic. A solution with a pH of 14 is very basic; one with a pH of 9 is mildly basic.

The pH of a substance can be found by using pH paper. The pH paper has been soaked in many different acid-base indicators. Litmus paper changes from one color to another at the neutralization point; a pH of 7. Other indicators change color at different pH levels.

In the next experiment, you can test the pH of a few substances.

EXPERIMENT 23

PH, A MEASURE OF HYDROGEN ION CONCENTRATION

You can find the pH of various substances using pH paper. As you can see from Table 9, pH measures the molar concentration of hydrogen ions (H^+). You can probably borrow some pH paper and the color scale that goes with it from your school's science department, or you can buy some at a science store, a hobby shop, or a pool supply company

THINGS YOU WILL NEED

- **science teacher or knowledgeable adult**
- **pH paper with color scale**
- **vinegar**
- **small jars or beakers**
- **water**
- **household ammonia**
- **cleanser powder (in water)**
- **baking soda (in water)**
- **lemon juice**
- **grape juice**
- **washing soda (in water)**
- **hydrochloric acid solution**
- **sodium hydroxide solution**

Table 8: The pH scale.

1	2	3	4	5	6	7	8	9	10	11	12	13	14
strong acid			weak acid			neutral			weak base				strong base

(pH paper is used to measure the acidity of swimming pool water).

1. Prepare small samples of the following substances in small jars or beakers: vinegar, ammonia, water, cleanser powder (dissolved in water), baking soda (dissolved in water), lemon juice, grape juice, and washing soda (dissolved in water).

2. Use pH paper and the color scale to determine the pH of the substances.

   The pH of water may not have been 7. Did that surprise you? Most water, including rain water, is slightly acidic.

3. What happens to the pH of vinegar if you dilute it by adding 10 mL (⅓ oz) of the vinegar to 90 mL (3 oz) of water?

4. What happens to the pH of the vinegar if you continue diluting it 1:10 with water? What happens to the pH of ammonia if you dilute it in the same way with water?

5. Ask your science teacher or a knowledgeable adult to help you find the pH of dilute (1.0 Molar)

pH	1	3	5	7	9	11	13	14
Molar concentration of H+ (moles/L)	10^{-1}	10^{-3}	10^{-5}	10^{-7}	10^{-9}	10^{-11}	10^{-13}	10^{-14}

Table 9. The concentration of hydrogen ions (H+) as indicated by pH.

hydrochloric acid and dilute (1.0 Molar) sodium hydroxide. What is the pH of this strong acid? Of this strong base?

Reexamine the data you collected in Experiment 17. Does pH (acidity or alkalinity) have any effect on the rate at which iron rusts?

EXPLORING ON YOUR OWN

• Use pH paper to measure the acidity of rain water. Is the pH of rain water affected by the season? For example, is summer rain more acidic than winter rain? What is the pH of snow? (You can let the snow melt and then find its pH.) In a long-lasting snow storm, is the pH of the first snow different than the pH of the last? If it is, how can you explain the difference?

• How does limestone ($CaCO_3$) affect the pH of water? Will the pH of water change if limestone is added to it? If it does, how can you explain it?

• Design and carry out an experiment to see how pH affects the germination of seeds.

EXPERIMENT 24

A LEAPING FLAME

Let's end with a fun experiment that you can use to entertain family and friends. Because you will be using matches and working with a burning candle, this chemical magic should be done **under adult supervision.**

THINGS YOU WILL NEED

- **an adult**
- **candle**
- **candle holder**
- **matches**
- **lamp chimney or large glass or plastic cylinder**

1. Light a candle. Let it burn for several minutes. Then blow out the candle.

2. Notice that a stream of light colored smoke continues to rise from the wick. The smoke is made of flammable hydrocarbon vapors from the wax.

3. Bring a lighted match to the stream of smoke several centimeters above the wick. The flame will follow the smoke stream downward and relight the wick.

4. If you do this experiment for an audience, the "magic" is best done with a clear chimney lamp or a glass or plastic cylinder over the candle as shown in Figure 20. The top of the cylinder can be about 10 cm (4 in) above the wick. This will make the distance that the flame jumps more dramatic.

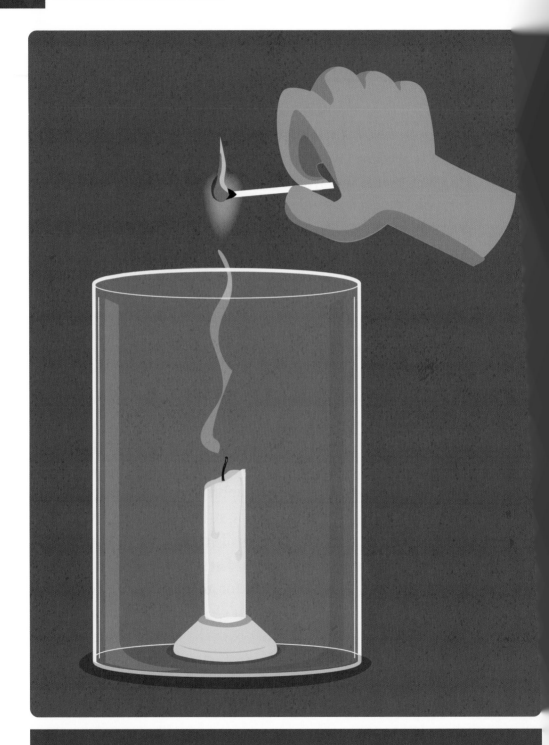

Figure 20. A leaping flame.

5. If done with an audience, announce that you will blow out the candle and relight it without bringing a match to the wick.
6. You then light a match, blow out the candle, and bring the match to the top of the chimney and the white vapor streaming from the wick.

    You can repeat this "magic" several times. But let the candle burn long enough so that there will be a good stream of vapor after the flame is blown out.

A PARTING THOUGHT

By doing the experiments in this book, you have learned much about chemistry. You have discovered ways to identify substances. You have investigated a variety of chemical reactions and the energy changes that occur in both physical and chemical changes. Along the way, you also encountered some fundamental scientific laws, such as the conservation of matter and energy, constant proportions, and multiple proportions.

If you have enjoyed these experiments and learning about chemistry, you may very well want to pursue a career as a chemist. There is a lot more to learn before you can call yourself a chemist, but we hope you now have a sense of what it involves. If a career as a chemist interests you, take chemistry, physics, and all the math courses offered in high school. Then, if chemistry still excites you, plan to major in chemistry in college. It could lead to a fascinating lifelong career.

GLOSSARY

acid—A compound that contains hydrogen that is released when the acid is added to certain metals, such as zinc. Acids turn blue litmus paper red, neutralize bases, and form hydrogen ions (H+) in water.

atom—The smallest particle of a chemical element.

atomic mass units (amu)—The relative mass of an atom of an element. For example, the relative mass of an oxygen atom is 16 amu; the relative mass of a hydrogen atom is 1 amu.

base—A substance that turns red litmus paper blue, has a bitter taste, and neutralizes acids.

chemical change—A chemical reaction in which the properties of the products are different from those of the reactants.

conservation of mass—Principle that states that during any change of state or chemical reaction as long as nothing is allowed to enter or leave, there is no change in mass.

conservation of mass-energy—Principle that states that the total amount of mass and energy in the universe is constant.

covalent chemical bonds—Bonds between atoms in compounds that are formed by sharing electrons.

density—The mass of a substance divided by its volume.

heat of fusion—The heat needed to melt one gram of a substance.

heat of vaporization—The heat needed to change one gram of a liquid at its boiling point to a gas.

ion—An atom that has a positive or negative charge.

law of definite proportions—Principle that states that elements that combine to form a compound always combine in a fixed ratio by weight.

law of multiple proportions—Principle that states that if two or more elements form more than one compound, the weight ratio of the elements in one compound will be a simple multiple of the weight ratio in the other compound or compounds.

mole—The atomic or molecular weight of an element or compound in amu expressed in grams.

molecule—The smallest particle of an element or compound that has the chemical properties of that element or compound.

oxidation-reduction—Oxidation is a loss of electrons; reduction is a gain of electrons. In this reaction, $Cu^{+2} + Fe \rightarrow Cu + Fe^{+2}$, iron (Fe) is oxidized and copper ions (Cu^{+2}) are reduced.

pH—A measure of the molar concentration of hydrogen ions (H+).

physical change—A change that does not lead to a change in the chemical makeup of matter. Changes of state or dissolving salt or sugar in water are examples of physical change.

polar molecules—Molecules in which one part of the molecule attracts electrons more strongly than other parts, causing the molecule to have slightly positive and negative regions.

FURTHER READING

BOOKS

Ardley, Neil. *101 Great Science Experiments.* New York, NY: DK Ltd., 2014.

Buczynski, Sandy. *Designing a Winning Science Fair Project.* Ann Arbor, MI: Cherry Lake Publishing, 2014.

Henneberg, Susan. *Creating Science Fair Projects with Cool New Digital Tools.* New York, NY: Rosen Central, 2014.

Margles, Samantha. *Mythbusters Science Fair Book.* New York, NY: Scholastic, 2011.

Mercer, Bobby. *Junk Drawer Chemistry: 50 Awesome Experiments that Don't Cost a Thing.* Chicago, IL: Chicago Review Press, 2015.

Navarro, Paula. *Incredible Experiments with Chemical Reactions and Mixtures.* Hauppauge, NY: Barron's Educational Series, 2014.

Thomas, Isabel. *Experiments with Materials.* Chicago, IL: Heinemann Raintree, 2016.

Wheeler-Toppen, Jodi. *Cool Chemistry Activities for Girls.* Mankato, MN: Capstone Press, 2012.

WEBSITES

ChemEd DL
chemeddl.org
A huge array of links to resources and chemistry communities.

Learn Chemistry
rsc.org/learn-chemistry
Resources for students and teachers of chemistry.

Master's in Data Science
*mastersindatascience.org/blog/the-ultimate-stem-guide-for-kids
   -239-cool-sites-about-science-technology-engineering-and
   -math*
Over 200 STEM links, including challenges and contests.

MIT Open Courseware
ocw.mit.edu/high-school
MIT's open resources for high school students interested in
   chemistry along with other sciences.

CAREER INFORMATION

ACS: Chemistry for Life

acs.org

Website for the American Chemical Society.

Big Future

bigfuture.collegeboard.org/majors-careers

A career and job-based website with a focus on college
majors.

Salary.com

swz.salary.com/SalaryWizard/Chemist-I-Job-Description.aspx

A place to find information on a variety of careers in
chemistry.

Science Pioneers

sciencepioneers.org/students/stem-websites

Links to various STEM career websites.

INDEX